TEN BOYS WHO USED
THEIR TALENTS

LIGHT KEEPERS

Irene Howat

CHRISTIAN FOCUS

© Copyright 2006 Christian Focus Publications
ISBN: 1-84550-146-2
Published by Christian Focus Publications Ltd,
Geanies House, Fearn, Tain, Ross-shire,
IV20 1TW, Scotland, Great Britain.
www.christianfocus.com
email:info@christianfocus.com
Cover design by Danie van Straaten
Cover illustration by Elena Temporin,
Milan Illustrations Agency

All incidents retold in these stories are based on true situations. Where specific information about childhood incidents has been unobtainable the author has written these paragraphs using other information concerning family life, hobbies, home life, relationships freely available in other biographies.

Printed and bound by
Nørhaven Paperback A/S

Cover illustration: Ghillean Prance and his mother used to row a boat on the loch near Dunvegan Castle on the Isle of Skye. His mother would sing Gaelic songs to attract the seals towards them. Ghillean's interest in nature was fostered from a very early age and when he became a Christian he truly appreciated the wonder of Creation.

Dedication
for Steven and Stuart

Contents

Wilfred Grenfell

'Kick it to me!' Wilfred yelled to his older brother.

Alfie dribbled the ball down the side of the football pitch, dodged the boy who was marking him, sighted his brother to his left and kicked the ball in his direction. Wilfred, being smaller and faster, ran with it between two members of the team they were playing, squared up to the net, and kicked for all he was worth.

'Goal!' several dozen boys screamed together. Even the supporters of the other team had to admit, it was a good one. After all, Wilfred was only ten years old.

'I want to be a footballer when I grow up,' he told his father.

Mr Grenfell smiled. 'That would be a turn-up for the books,' he said. 'We've had ministers in the family; we've had teachers in the family, but we've not yet had a footballer.'

'But I don't need to be a minister or a teacher, do I?' Wilfred asked, horrified at the thought. 'I mean, I can still be a Grenfell and do something else, can't I?'

'Of course you can,' laughed his father. 'But it would be good if we could see you putting effort into your schoolwork. Remember, footballers need to count their goals.'

Wilfred was not stupid, nor was he lazy. His problem was purely and simply that he couldn't sit still. Had his teachers allowed him to move about in the class he might well have done better in his young days at school. But, in 1875, when Wilfred scored his best goal so far, school desks were in straight lines, and boys were expected to have straight backs and silent tongues in the classroom.

'What are you doing, Wilfred?' his teacher asked one day, when he noticed that his pupil was more interested in something on the floor than in what he was being taught.

'I'm sorry, Sir,' the boy said. 'I was watching an earwig.'

'Perhaps you would like to come and tell the class about earwigs then.'

Wilfred was on his feet in an instant.

'The common earwig is between half and three-quarters of an inch long, and brown. It's the most common member of the *Dermaptera* family and its Latin name is *Forficula auricularia*. Although earwigs like dark places, there is no real evidence that they enter the human ear other than by chance.'

Had the teacher not been new to the class he would have been less surprised. All Wilfred's friends knew that he could talk all morning about insects.

Alfie, who was very clever with his hands, made wooden cases in which Wilfred could display the insects he collected. Each specimen was caught carefully in order not to damage it. But, sadly, each insect that reached his beautifully arranged collection was well and truly dead.

'What do we have here?' asked Mr Grenfell, looking at a set of butterflies. 'I know this one. Isn't it a tortoiseshell?'

'That's right. It's *Aglais urticae*. The tortoiseshell butterfly is common all summer in England; then it hibernates from October until April, depending on the weather.'

'And the others in your collection?'

'The next one is the Red Admiral, *Vanessa atalanta*, which arrives here from the Mediterranean in late Spring. Red Admirals eat nettles. We often see them on the buddleia bush in the garden.'

'I suppose that's why buddleia is nicknamed the butterfly bush,' Alfie said.

'Got it in one,' laughed Wilfred.

'I think we should forget the insect collection for an afternoon and plan our next sail,' suggested Alfie, who then began singing an old sea shanty about a drunken sailor.

'Somehow I don't think it would be a good idea to be drunk and a sailor,' laughed his brother. 'If you were sailing a boat as small as our one, you'd probably end up very wet indeed, maybe even very drowned!'

'Let's have a look at the map.'

Mr Grenfell watched his two growing-up sons. Why was it, he wondered, that Wilfred could discuss insects in great detail – and in Latin – when he had very little interest in his school subjects. And how was it that he could spend ages studying maps with a view to planning sails during the holidays when he wasn't interested in his geography lessons?

'I may be a headmaster,' the man thought, 'but I don't think I understand my younger son very well at all.'

'What a cough you have,' Wilfred's teacher said. 'You should see the school matron.'

It was 1881. The boy was 16 years old and a pupil at Marlborough School in Wiltshire.

'Take this,' Matron said, giving him a spoonful of foul-tasting brown liquid. 'A few doses of this will soon sort you out.'

'Or kill me,' thought Wilfred. 'It's Disgusting with a capital D!'

But the medicine did not cure the cough, which grew worse and worse.

'Here's Wilfred coming,' his friends said, before he came into sight. 'I'd know that cough anywhere.'

Taking their doctor's advice, Wilfred's parents sent him off to stay with his aunt in the South of France.

'The warm air there will do him the world of good,' said the doctor. 'A term away from school won't cause any problems, I'm sure.'

Mr Grenfell wasn't quite so sure. He just shook his head when he thought of Wilfred's school marks, and the regular 'Could try harder' and 'Could do better' that was written in his exercise books.

'I'm having a wonderful time,' Wilfred wrote home to Alfie. 'Aunt's friend has two teenage daughters and they're so interested in nature study. Yesterday we collected frogs from the wild and brought them into the miniature ponds in the garden. Mind you, we've had to put nets over the ponds to keep the frogs in. And there are butterflies here that I've never seen in England. How many different butterflies do you think there are? I'll bring some specimens back with me... if I can ever tear myself away from here to come home.'

But come home he did, not best pleased to be back at school.

'What are you going to do with your life?' Mr Grenfell asked his son when he was eighteen years old.

'I've decided to be a doctor,' he said. 'That's what I'm going to do.'

'A doctor? We've never had a Doctor Grenfell in the family,' his father replied. 'Do you know how much studying that involves?'

Wilfred found training to be a doctor very hard work indeed. His head was fairly buzzing with medical information as he walked along a London street in 1885. Suddenly he heard the sound of singing, and he followed it into a huge tent.

'Who's he?' the young man wondered. Then he remembered hearing about a famous American preacher called D.L. Moody and that he was in town.

During the meeting a man prayed a very long prayer. Wilfred was becoming so bored that he was about to leave when he was amazed by Mr Moody, who interrupted the prayer, saying, 'Let us sing a hymn while our brother finishes his prayer.'

Wilfred stayed! By the time he left that meeting he had come to know the Lord Jesus Christ as his Saviour. As he walked home, Wilfred decided to try to be the kind of doctor Jesus Christ would want him to be.

Not too long afterwards, Wilfred was in the middle of a bunch of noisy young boys. He shook his head and smiled. His minister had asked him if he wanted to be a Sunday school teacher. 'Yes, I'd love to!' he'd exclaimed. Now he was finding out that teaching noisy young lads wasn't as easy as he had thought.

'Sit down and listen,' he told his class, over and over again.

But they seemed quite unable to sit still.

'What are they like?' Wilfred said to himself, after one particularly noisy class and the answer came into his mind right away. 'They're exactly the same as I was. What they need is to get rid of some energy before they'll sit and listen.'

That was how the East End Boys' Club was born. Not only did they have games together at their weekly meetings, they also went sailing with Wilfred and Alfie, and had a marvellous time. They learned that it was good to train their bodies to serve the Lord as well as training their minds and souls.

No sooner was Wilfred back in London than he realised how much he missed the sea.

'I really don't like big cities,' he thought. 'In fact, I'm not at my happiest on dry land at all. But I don't suppose there are many medical practices at sea!'

Not long afterwards there was a surprise in store for Dr Wilfred Grenfell.

'I think I know of a job that would suit you very well' said Dr Treves. 'I'm a member of the National Mission to Deep Sea Fishermen. We're looking for a doctor to help with the work. We're presently equipping a medical ship and we need a doctor on board to serve the deep sea fishermen in the North Sea.'

Wilfred's pulse raced as his heart beat fast with excitement.

'It won't be easy,' added Dr Treves. 'Deep sea fishermen can be a rough lot of men.'

Easy or difficult, this was the job for Dr Wilfred Grenfell. He took the train to Yarmouth where the *Thomas Gray* was being fitted out as a medical ship. It looked grand tied up to the quay, but it seemed smaller and frailer a few months later when, in 1888, after a stormy sea voyage across the Atlantic, the crew first sighted the fishing fleet.

'Hoist the blue banner,' the captain shouted. 'That'll let them know we're here.'

Before long Wilfred's first patients were being helped to transfer from trawlers that had drawn alongside.

There were horrible burns from fires on the wooden ships, broken bones held together with makeshift splints, rotten teeth to be extracted, injuries from drunken falls and brawls, as well as all sorts of illnesses.

Once men's medical needs were seen to, they were offered books to read, a brief rest and a change of clothes.

They also heard about the Lord Jesus Christ and how he could save their souls for heaven. Life at sea was rough and tough, and the *Thomas Gray* was a welcome addition to the fleet.

For three years Wilfred worked among the fishermen. On shore he went round churches telling people about the work of the National Mission to Deep Sea Fishermen.

'I could almost feel the wind whistling through my hair,' one lady said, after hearing him speak.

'And I began to feel sea-sick,' her friend laughed. 'I've never heard anyone tell such vivid stories. We really must give some money to help with Dr Grenfell's work.'

In 1892, after hearing about the fishermen who spent all year round off the coast of Newfoundland, Wilfred felt the Lord was leading him there. As they sailed towards St John's, a strange light lit the sky.

'It looks like the whole town's on fire,' one of the sailors said. And it was. Reaching harbour as quickly as they could, they set out to help in the devastation. Wilfred had plenty of burns patients that day.

'We needed you, Doctor,' the governor of the colony said, by way of thanks.

And that's just what Wilfred felt. There were plenty of doctors in England. He was needed here.

From St John's, in Newfoundland, Wilfred headed north among the difficult currents, icebergs, fjords and cliffs of Labrador. In one settlement after another he found people in need of his help.

'We've never had a doctor here,' he was told, and he could see that himself from badly set bones, wounds that wouldn't heal, and young people old beyond their years.

He knew they'd never had a minister either, so as he worked as a doctor, he also chatted to people about the Lord.

During the years that followed Wilfred worked among the fishermen and visited settlements. But, in 1899, he decided that Labrador was where he should be rather than among the fishermen. In the summers Wilfred sailed up and down the wild coastline. Winters were spent travelling by dog sled. Once, in April 1908, when he was on his way through thick ice to reach a boy who was ill, he and his dogs were trapped on ice that broke off and floated out to sea! Three of his dogs lost their lives that day in order that Wilfred and his other dogs could be saved.

'That was six months ago,' Wilfred concluded, having told a group of Christians back in England about his adventure. 'God was very good to me that day.'

God was also good to him on the voyage back to Labrador, for that was when he met Anne MacClanahan, who became his wife. He spent much of that voyage telling her what his hopes and dreams were for Labrador.

Years later Wilfred and his wife revisited those dreams.

'Just think of it,' he said, smiling. 'It's

1927, and the International Grenfell Mission has helped to build six hospitals, five schools, nine nursing stations and an orphanage.'

'And it has allowed women to sell the crafts they make over the long winter months. Some of their lovely work is on the other side of the Atlantic Ocean now,' Anne smiled.

'Most important of all,' Wilfred added, 'men, women, boys and girls have heard about Jesus, and many have put their faith in him.'

Anne smiled. 'There are people in this cold, wild place who feel as though they've walked along the warm sandy shores of the Sea of Galilee, for I've never heard a story-teller like you. Of course, that's also why the Mission has been able to do so much. When you tell people in Britain or America about the hardships in Labrador and Newfoundland, they feel so chilled and hungry and ill that they're willing to open their hearts and their wallets to give money for the work to go on.'

The work did go on, even after Wilfred Grenfell died in 1940, two years after his wife.

Fact File: Discovery
John Cabot, in the ship *Matthew*, first sighted the lands of Labrador and Newfoundland on June 24th 1497. In the year 1583 Sir Humphrey Gilbert reached the harbour of St. John's with letters from Queen Elizabeth I authorising him to take possession of Newfoundland.

Keynote: Wilfred Grenfell wasn't that great a scholar. He would rather kick a football around than sit still in class. Earwigs were more interesting than algebra. But he knew a lot about the natural world and showed himself to be intelligent as well as hard working. Sometimes we can feel that we aren't as successful as we could be. Perhaps we wish we were smarter or that we knew more facts? God has given us all different abilities. Some people are smart and organised, some are good at looking after others. Wilfred was good with practical, hands-on things. We should thank God for our abilities. We shouldn't covet the talents that other people have. Instead, we should work hard at developing those talents God has given us.

Think: When Wilfred was asked what he was going to do with his life he said that he was going to be a doctor. His father reminded him that he would have to do a lot of study – and Wilfred wasn't well known for being a good student. However, he did his best although it was hard at first. For years God had been preparing him for mission work at sea and in inhospitable regions. Think about what God is preparing you for – right at this moment. You may go on to study at college or university, you may take up a trade or learn a skill. You may even have a hobby or favourite pastime that God is planning to use in the future to bring others to trust in his Son, Jesus Christ.

 Prayer: Lord Jesus, thank you for gifts and talents. Thank you that you are planning my future and that I am safe with you, whatever happens. Help me to use my time, strengths, body and mind – everything about me – to honour you. Amen.

C.S. Lewis

'Dinner time!' Mum called. 'Come on Clive, or it will be cold.'

Four-year-old Clive was looking at a picture book. He found it so interesting that he didn't even hear his mother calling. Warnie, his older brother, was sent to fetch him.

'Come on,' he said. 'I'm starving.'

'I'll just finish this book,' Clive replied. 'There are only three more pages.'

Warnie decided to resort to serious tactics. 'There's a spider climbing up the back of your chair,' he said quietly.

His little brother was off the chair and in his mother's arms in a split second. He hated spiders. In fact, Clive's definition of a nightmare was to dream about spiders!

'Don't do that, please,' said Mrs Lewis to Warnie, when she eventually calmed Clive down enough to hear what had happened. 'You're three years older than he is, quite big enough to know not to give your brother a fright.'

'But I was hungry,' wailed Warnie. 'And dinner would have been cold if we'd waited till he'd finished the book.'

Mr Lewis shook his head. 'It's cold anyway with all this fussation.'

Just a few weeks later Clive was in tears again, this time for a very good reason.

'Why did Jacksie get run over by a car? Why didn't the car stop?' the boy wept. 'I loved him. He was the very best dog in the whole wide world.'

'I'm sorry, dear,' said his mother, holding him in her arms. 'I'm afraid the car driver didn't have time to stop when Jacksie ran out in front of him. It really wasn't his fault.'

For days Clive talked of nothing but Jacksie, and for weeks he kept forgetting he had been run over and would expect him to come, tail wagging, for a rough and tumble.

Then, quite out of the blue, Clive made an announcement.

'My name's not Clive now. I'm called Jacksie. And if anyone calls me Clive, I'll not answer.'

Although he was only four, Clive had made up his mind. He totally refused to answer to any other name from then on. He was Jacksie, then Jacks, and eventually Jack for the rest of his life. However, he used his real name when he became an author. Today he's known as C.S. Lewis. As that is how he's remembered, we'll call him C.S. for the rest of this story.

'Does Warnie need to go away to school?' C.S. asked his father.

'I'm afraid that's what we've decided,' Mr Lewis said. 'We think the school we've chosen in Watford is the best place for him to go.'

C.S. wailed, 'But that's across the sea in England?'

'My dear boy,' smiled his father. 'You make Belfast sound as though it's at the South Pole. England is just a short sail across the Irish Sea.'

'Watford feels as far away as the South Pole,' C.S. sulked. 'I just don't want Warnie to go. I'll miss him.'

C.S. missed his brother very much indeed because the boys were very good friends. Warnie's absence allowed more time for reading, and among his favourite books were those written by Beatrix Potter.

'Look at Peter Rabbit's blue jacket,' he said to his mother. 'Do you remember the story of Benjamin Bunny, when Peter lost his jacket and was wrapped up in a red cotton handkerchief?'

Both Mrs Lewis and C.S. knew the story so well that they were able to say it by heart together.

'Peter was sitting by himself. He looked poorly, and was dressed in a red cotton pocket-handkerchief. "Peter," said little Benjamin, in a whisper, "who has got your clothes?"'

Mother and son fell into a fit of giggles.

'I think you should put on your jacket now,' said his mother. 'It's a nice day for a walk.'

But C.S.'s time at home was as short as Warnie's, and he joined his brother at school in England when he was nine years old. The following year their mother died.

'Are we going to Boxen today?' Warnie asked his young brother one Saturday afternoon. They had done their team games and were free till teatime.

'Yes please,' C.S. grinned. 'I like Boxen better than here.'

Boxen was their imaginary world. Its inhabitants were animals, and its rulers were animals too. Teachers and pupils, kings and servants, soldiers and fishermen – all were animals.

C.S. suggested, 'How about designing a Boxen army uniform. I think it should be a royal blue jacket with silver epaulettes and buttons, and dark blue trousers with a silver stripe down the sides.'

'What will they wear on their heads?' asked Warnie.

'You choose,' C.S. said. 'I chose everything else.'

Although Boxen was an imaginary place it seemed very real indeed to the brothers, and they loved pretending to go there.

Being a soldier was not a game in 1917 when C.S. joined the Somerset Light Infantry the year before the end of the First World War. He arrived in the terrible Somme Valley in France on his 19th birthday. Paddy Moore, C.S.'s best friend, was killed in action. Before the war C.S. had studied at Oxford University for a year. After he recovered from his war wounds he returned there to study.

'Do you believe in God?' C.S. was asked by one of his friends, after he became a Fellow of Magdalen College, Oxford, where he taught.

'I did as a boy,' he replied. 'But then I lost what faith I had. And it would have been hard to believe in a loving God in the Somme. In a strange way I think I feel angry at God for not existing because I think he should.'

C.S. shuddered at the memory of his war years. Every time he thought back to the Somme he remembered Paddy, the young man who, like millions of others, never came home.

'What are you writing?' Warnie asked his brother. 'Another poem?'

'Yes, actually,' C.S. replied. 'Another poem.'

'It looks rather long for a poem,' teased Warnie. 'Are you sure it's not a detective story?'

C.S. was writing a very long poem. In fact, it was so long it was published as a book!

'You writers,' Warnie laughed. 'Look at the length of books your friend Tolkien writes.'

'Don't his Hobbits remind you of Boxen and the characters we invented to live there?' C.S. asked.

'Of course they do,' his brother laughed. 'If you'd taken up writing sooner you might have written *The Lord of the Rings* yourself!'

Among C.S. Lewis's friends were a number of Christians, and the men often had long discussions together. What they said, and the kind of lives they lived, made C.S. think very seriously.

'I give in,' he said eventually, in 1929. 'I admit that God is God.'

Having admitted that in his mind, C.S. Lewis knelt and prayed. But it was another two years before he became a Christian.

'Let's visit Whipsnade Zoo,' suggested Warnie in 1931. 'We'll go on my motorbike and you can travel in the sidecar.'

It was a sunny morning as the pair of them sped from Oxford, south towards London. C.S., sitting in the sidecar, had time to think as he looked at the countryside through which they were passing. And something happened during that journey that changed his life. He had news for Warnie at Whipsnade.

'When we set out,' he said, 'I did not believe that Jesus is the Son of God and when we reached the zoo I did.'

By then Warnie and C.S. had bought The Kilns, a large house near Oxford, and this they shared with Paddy Moore's mother.

'I just love it here,' said Warnie, as the brothers walked through the grounds.

'It has everything: tennis court, a pond, woods and an orchard – eight acres of England that's ours to enjoy.'

When the Second World War broke out children from the cities were sent to the countryside for safety. They were called evacuees. In September 1939, several of them arrived at The Kilns. The quietness there seemed very strange to them after the hustle and bustle of London.

'Do you really swim in that pond?' one of them asked C.S.

'Every morning,' he replied. 'I go out in the punt to the middle then dive in – first asking the moorhens to move over and make room, of course.'

'Yuck!' said another. 'The water's brown!'

'And when I come out I'm pink,' laughed C.S. Lewis. 'Or blue, if it's wintertime. Let me tell you a story about the birds and animals that live in and around the pond.'

'You're good at telling stories,' a girl said.

'Course he is,' snapped her friend. 'He writes books, doesn't he?'

There was never any argument if C.S. offered to tell the evacuees a story. They were always willing to curl up around his chair and listen.

'That's an interesting old wardrobe,' commented one of the evacuees. Then she grinned mischievously. 'May we go inside and see if there's anything behind it?'

'By all means,' said C.S. Lewis.

As the children scrambled into the oversized wardrobe memories of Boxen came into C.S.'s head. 'I wonder,' he thought. 'There might be the beginnings of a story right here in the wardrobe.'

C.S. Lewis worked at Oxford University for twenty-nine years, and over that time he wrote many books. Some were very learned, others were stories, and many taught about Jesus Christ. It was in 1950 that his famous children's books began to be published.

'I have our evacuee children to thank for the idea,' he thought, when *The Lion, the Witch and the Wardrobe,* was published. 'They made me think of a world behind a wardrobe.' Then he smiled. 'But I suppose it really goes further back than that – right back to Boxen and the characters Warnie and I invented for our secret world.'

In 1954, C.S. Lewis moved from Oxford to become a professor at Cambridge University.

'How many Narnia books have you written?' a boy asked C.S. Lewis the following year. 'I've collected the first four, and I'm saving up for the others.'

The author thought for a moment. 'So you have *The Lion, the Witch and the Wardrobe, Prince Caspian, The Voyage of the Dawn Treader* and *The Silver Chair*.'

'That's right,' nodded the lad.

'And you've still to get *The Horse and his Boy, The Magician's Nephew* and *The Last Battle*.'

The child's eyes shone. 'Wow! You mean I have three more still to read?'

'I tell you what,' said C.S. Lewis. 'You give me your address and I'll send you a copy of *The Horse and his Boy*, then you'll only have to save up for another two.'

'Oh thank you,' he grinned. 'Thank you ever so much!'

'May I ask you a question before I go?' said the boy.

'You've already asked me one,' C.S. laughed. 'But feel free to ask another.'

It took a minute for him to realise what he meant, then he could hardly speak for giggling.

'In the Narnia books, is Aslan meant to be Jesus?'

'That, my lad, is a very big question. Why do you ask?'

The child screwed up his face as he tried to think what he meant.

'It's just that Aslan did the things Jesus did. He overcame evil and he rose from the dead too. And he seems ... so ... beautiful and good and so powerful.'

C.S. looked very serious. 'If you think Aslan is like Jesus then the Narnia stories will be more than just stories to you. You will understand them in a special way. But remember, Jesus is not like Aslan. Jesus is higher and holier and much more amazing than any storybook character could ever be.'

Although C.S. Lewis wrote many books for children, he had no children of his own. He shared his home with Warnie and Paddy Moore's mother until Mrs Moore died in 1951. Shortly after her death he met an American writer, Joy Gresham, who had two young sons. Five years later C.S. and Joy were married. For the first time, the storyteller had boys at home to tell stories to. Sadly, Joy only lived for three years after they were married.

When the boy to whom C.S. Lewis had sent the book was some years older, he read *The Lion the Witch and the Wardrobe* to his young brother. This is my favourite bit, he said, as he turned over a very worn page.

'Aslan stood up and when he opened his mouth to roar his face became so terrible that they did not dare to look at it. And they saw all the trees in front of him bend down before the blast of his roaring as grass bends in a meadow before the wind. Then he said, "We have a long journey to go. You must ride on me." And he crouched down and the children climbed on to his warm, golden back. ... That ride was perhaps the most wonderful thing that happened to them in Narnia. ... This is a mount that doesn't need to be guided and never grows tired.'

The boy remembered what C.S. Lewis had said, and saw a deeper meaning. A psalm from the Bible came into his mind. 'My help comes from the Lord, ... he who watches over Israel will neither slumber nor sleep.'

In November 1963, he heard on the news that C.S. Lewis had died. And the young man remembered the quiet storyteller he had once met, and whom he would never ever forget.

Fact File: Chronicles of Narnia
C.S. Lewis' books are famous the world over. The final title in the Chronicles of Narnia, *The Last Battle* won the Carnegie Medal for Children's Literature. C.S. Lewis dedicated *The Horse and His Boy* to David and Douglas Gresham who were later to become his stepsons. Lewis didn't just write children's books. *Surprised by Joy* is the autobiography of his early life that focuses on his conversion.

Keynote: C.S. Lewis had an amazing imagination. As a child he and his brother invented imaginary worlds to live in. Years later Lewis would invent another world called Narnia. Our imagination is a gift from God. We may not write books or poems but we can be creative in other ways. We should take care of our minds and bodies. Our imagination can be tarnished if we keep looking at things that do not please God. Our bodies can be damaged and spoiled if we do not follow God's laws.

Think: Lewis was asked if he believed in God. He answered that he had done once. He had questions and doubts and couldn't understand how there could be a God of love when he remembered the awful fighting during the First World War. There is a lot of evil in the world. Today we can see war on our T.V. screens. Perhaps you wonder how a God of love could allow such awful disasters to happen throughout the world? When you think about how the world began and how it all went wrong, then you will realise that the horrible things that happen in our lives are a result of sin. Our disobedience of God has spoiled the beautiful world. It is only Jesus Christ who can deliver us from sin and bring us back to a right relationship with God.

 Prayer: Lord God, when we have questions and doubts about you help us to bring our worries to you. Help us to read your Word so that we can learn and know the truth. Help us to find out about you and about who you really are – a merciful, faithful and just God.

James Clerk Maxwell

James stood by the front door of his home locking then unlocking the door key. Each time the key turned he listened for the click and tried to picture what was happening in the bit of the lock that he couldn't see. Deciding to discover if the puzzle was any clearer from the other side, the four-year-old opened the heavy door and was about to go out.

'Come away from there,' said a voice behind him. 'We don't want you wandering out to the stream. There was so much rain last night that there's more than enough water to wash away a young boy like yourself.'

Slowly James turned round, for his mind was still on the puzzle of the lock.

'I'll not go near the stream,' he told Maggie. 'I'm just going on to the doorstep to look at the outside of the lock.'

'You're a strange boy, and no mistake,' Maggie said. 'I've looked after children all of my working life, and I've never met one like you for wanting to know how things work.'

'Good morning Ma'am,' Maggie smiled, when James's mother appeared on the scene. 'The young master is about his investigations again.'

Mrs Maxwell smiled down at her lad. For someone so small, she thought, he was interested in a great many things.

'Is it time for my lessons?' James asked.

'I think we'll do nature study today,' said his mother, who was also his teacher. 'Some interesting things may have been washed down the stream in the storm last night. Let's go and see what we can find.'

Wrapping her cloak around her, Mrs Maxwell walked down the path to the trees at the foot of the front garden of Glenlair and watched as her son clambered down the bank to the stream that ran through the trees.

'I love nature study,' the boy said, picking up a sparkly stone and holding it like a special treasure.

'You know what I've told you over and over again,' his mother reminded him. 'Look up ...'

James joined in, for he knew exactly what she was going to say. 'Look up through nature to nature's God.'

'Who made the sparkly stone?' asked Mrs Maxwell.

'God did,' he laughed. Then, as he looked around at the rolling hills of Kirkcudbrightshire, in the southwest of

Scotland, he added, 'God made everything I can see, and all the things I've still to discover.'

'We have visitors today,' said Mrs Maxwell, three years later. 'Mrs McMillan is coming with Thomas. Think of a game to play.'

James was ready with his favourite toy when the carriage arrived at the door.

'What's that?' asked Thomas, who lived in the nearby village of Twynholm.

'It's my magic spinner,' James explained. 'If you watch it when it spins you'll see a story.'

Puzzled at the very idea, Thomas watched as James spun the disk that was covered with drawings he had done. At first it looked like a blur of grey. Then, quite suddenly when it was spinning quickly enough, he could see a dog jumping over a gate. All the little pictures James had drawn merged into a moving story!

'Are you going to do any tricks today?' Thomas asked later.

James, who had been teaching his dog tricks, held up three fingers. 'How many fingers am I holding up?' he asked.

Toby barked three times.

'And how many this time?'

Toby barked ten times, and James was holding up ten fingers.

37

'Let me try,' said Thomas, holding up four fingers.

There was silence for a few seconds, and then Toby barked once. James wouldn't tell his friend how to make Toby count. He only told his mother after a great deal of persuasion.

'I taught him to bark each time I blink. So if I hold up seven fingers I blink seven times, and he barks seven times.'

A dark cloud crept over James Clerk Maxwell's happy childhood in 1838 when he was just seven. His mother, who was also his teacher, companion and friend, became ill. She still taught him, especially from the Bible. By the time he was eight years old he could say the whole of the 119th psalm by heart – all 176 verses of it!

'I've brought you some tadpoles,' James said, as he went into his mother's room. 'Look, Mum, you can see their squiggly wiggly tails. I think nature's wonderful.'

Mrs Maxwell, who spent most of her time in bed now, looked at the jar of tadpoles and smiled. 'If you forget everything else I've taught you, James,' she said, 'don't forget this. Look up through nature to nature's God.'

Something told James that what had been said was of terrific importance. 'I will, Mum,' he said. 'I promise you that I will.'

And it was not long afterwards that Mr Maxwell told his son that his mother had gone to heaven.

'Oh, I'm so glad,' James said. 'Now she'll have no more pain.'

Thinking that he was doing the best thing for James, Mr Maxwell hired a tutor to teach him at home. Had he known what an unkind man the tutor was, James's father would never have given him the job. In fact, he was so unkind that James often ran away from him.

'Oh! Come and see this!' Maggie yelled to the other servants, 'Come to the window and see this. If it wasn't so pathetic it would be funny.'

James had run away from his tutor to the pond in the garden. Having put a half-barrel into the water, the boy had climbed into it and paddled out to the middle of the pond. His tutor grabbed a garden rake and was reaching as far as he could to try to haul his pupil back, but James always managed to paddle just out of reach.

'I hope the horrible man falls in,' said Jeannie, the kitchen maid.

'And I would hope that too if it wouldn't put him in a worse mood than ever.'

It took two years before Mr Maxwell realised how unhappy his son was. But, when he did, the unkind tutor was sent packing. And so was James, who was sent to school in Edinburgh. He wasn't alone in the city, for he stayed with his aunt there. Laughed at because of his country clothes, and teased because of his Kirkcudbrightshire accent, James found school annoying and boring and spent the weeks looking forward to his father's Saturday visits.

'I've a treat for you today,' Mr Maxwell said, one Saturday. 'We're going to a lecture at the Edinburgh Royal Society.'

'What's that?' James asked, but his father just grinned and told him it was all about wasp.

'What about wasp?' the twelve-year-old asked, thinking his dad was talking nonsense.

'How do you spell wasp?' asked Mr Maxwell.

'W ... a ... s ... p.'

'That's right,' the man laughed. 'W is for wait, a is for and, s is for see and p is for please. So wasp is short for wait and see please.'

'I'll remember that,' James laughed. 'Aunt always says I've to wait and see when I ask what's for dinner. Next time I'll tell her we're eating wasps.'

The Edinburgh Royal Society lectures were often on very interesting scientific subjects, and they became the highlight of

James Clerk Maxwell's young life. When he was fourteen, a paper he wrote was read to the Society. It had to be read by a university professor because James was thought to be too young to read it himself.

In 1847, when he was sixteen years old, James became a student at Edinburgh University. But after a while there Mr Maxwell realised that it would be better for his son to go to Cambridge University to get a thorough grounding in mathematics. The thing that bothered him most was that Cambridge was not well known for its Christian approach to science. After much thought, and no doubt many prayers, Mr Maxwell agreed that James should move south, to Cambridge. There he continued experimenting with anything and everything that came to hand.

'What are you doing?' his friend asked him one day, having watched James take the college cat into his room every day for over a week. 'Are you troubled with mice?'

James laughed and told his friend that he was doing an experiment, and to come and see. Sitting down, he watched James lift the cat 30 cm off the ground then drop it. The cat's feet were up in air but the cat spun round and landed on its feet. Next time, he dropped the cat from 25 cm off the ground. Again the cat spun round and landed on its feet.

'You are quite mad!' his friend laughed.

'Not at all,' said James, grinning. 'I've even proved that a cat dropped from just 5 cm above ground level can twist round and land on its feet. Now, isn't that interesting?'

While a student, James's mother's words often came into his mind as he did his experiments. 'Look up through nature to nature's God.' But instead of just accepting what his mother had taught him, James examined everything with a scientist's eye, and found for himself that he believed in God, the God who made the wonderful world that he so much enjoyed exploring.

Having completed his studies in Cambridge James Clerk Maxwell moved in 1856 to Aberdeen in North East Scotland where he taught in Marischal College. James was not a brilliant lecturer, possibly because his mind moved too fast, but after lectures his students loved to stay behind because he did experiments with them. They could understand him better then! Science was not the only thing James enjoyed at Marischal College, because that's where he met Mary Dewar – her father was College Principal – they fell in love and were married. Even before they married they studied the Bible together, and they continued that throughout their married life.

Four years after moving to Aberdeen, James and Mary went to live in London when James became Professor of Physics and Astronomy at King's College. For a long time James had been interested in the planet Saturn, and in the rings that surround it.

'How is it that the rings around Saturn hold their shape?' a student asked.

Another student shook his head. 'There are so many theories about that, I don't know which to believe.'

'Well,' said Professor James Clerk Maxwell, 'from a maths and physics perspective, the only way that Saturn's rings can remain as stable as they are is if they are made up of numerous small solid particles rather than being formed from gases.'

The students knew not to argue, and went off to think about what their professor had said. Nothing has been discovered since then to disprove Maxwell's theory of Saturn's rings.

James Clerk Maxwell's main area of interest became electricity and magnetism.

'I owe so much to Michael Faraday,' Maxwell told his students. 'What I have discovered is based on what he discovered before me. That is the nature of science. Each discovery builds on what has gone before.'

'What part of Mr Faraday's work most interests you?' he was asked.

43

Maxwell's eyes lit up. 'I'm working on his theories of electricity and magnetism, and how electricity travels through space. But it is a massive piece of research. It will take years to complete ... if I live long enough.'

In 1865 James and his wife moved back to Glenlair, his family home, where he set up a laboratory and continued his experiments free from the teaching commitments he had in the south. For the following six years he worked on electricity and magnetism. During those years he went, from time to time, to Cambridge to meet with fellow scientists working in the same field. Then in 1871 he moved back to Cambridge where he became Professor of Physics.

'No one has explained the laws of magnetism and electricity as Maxwell has,' a man in the Edinburgh Royal Society said to a friend. 'His mathematical brain has done a fine job. Who else but a mathematician could have calculated that the speed of propagation of an electromagnetic field is approximately the speed of light, and that light is therefore an electromagnetic phenomenon. The light we can see is, consequently, only a small part of the entire spectrum of electromagnetic activity.'

'Excuse me,' said his friend. 'You're talking to an ordinary human being, not a scientist.'

The man laughed 'All right,' he said. 'In words that any mere mortal will understand, I believe that James Clerk Maxwell's calculations and experiments have opened the door to things that we cannot even begin to imagine, but which will be common 100 years from now. And the interesting thing is that he has no time whatever for those who tell us that all we see around us has evolved rather than having been created. I heard him say in a lecture that we should look through nature to the God of nature. And what wonderful things he has discovered by doing just that.'

That man was to be proved quite right. Although James Clerk Maxwell's theories are difficult to understand, his work provided the basis from which we now have radio, television, radar and satellite communications.

Fact File: King's College
James Clerk Maxwell became Professor of Physics and Astronomy at King's College, London. This college was founded by King George IV and the Duke of Wellington (then Prime Minister) in 1829. Two other famous people who attended this college were John Keats the poet, and Florence Nightingale. James' work in the field of electricity and magnetism was a continuation of another scientist's work. This man was Michael Faraday, who was also a Christian.

Keynote: James' mum told him to look through nature to the God of nature. The Bible tells us this too. In Psalm 19: 1 it says, 'The heavens declare the glory of God.' Look at the world around you with fresh eyes. You will see wonderful scenery and amazing animals, birds and plant life. There are fields and gardens, mountains and jungles and some places that human beings haven't even discovered yet – and they were all made by the Lord God.

Think: Think about a beautiful bird and then think about how intricate it is. Look in the mirror – you may not think you look that stunning – but think for a minute about the eyes you are using to look at yourself. They are amazing. We see thousands of different images on a daily basis as well as being able to see things near and far. There are so many colours that our eyes can pick out. Can you honestly believe that these wonderful things were made by chance? Of course not – they were designed. Creation proves to us the existence of the Creator.

 Prayer: Lord Jesus, we know that you are our caring creator and that we have you to thank for our wonderful world. It is amazing that you, the all powerful creator, came to earth as a tiny, helpless baby, and that you died on the cross to save your people from their sins. We worship you and praise you for this wonderful truth.

Ghillean Prance

Dunvegan Castle looked enormous from the small boat on the loch. Ghillean looked at its ramparts against the deep blue sky and smiled.

'What are you thinking about?' his mother asked, returning his smile.

Ghillean looked from the castle to the sparking waters of the loch, and to the seals sunning themselves on a rock before he answered.

'I was thinking that this must be the best place in the world,' said the boy. 'There is so much to see and do.'

Mrs Prance, who was staying with her cousin at Dunvegan House, just along the loch from the great castle, agreed with her six-year-old son.

'And if this is the best place in the world, what would be the best thing you could do right now?' the woman asked.

Ghillean grinned. He didn't need to think about the answer to that question.

'I'd like you to sing a song to the seals that would make them come alongside.'

Very quietly Mrs Prance sang a Gaelic song, fitting the rhythm of the song to the slow movement of the oars. Two seals turned their heads in her direction and seemed to stop to think if they should be bothered moving. Then, as though the same thought entered both their minds, they lumbered into the water and swam towards the boat.

The boy watched entranced as they followed the boat, caught up in the beauty of his mother's song. The Gaelic air ended, and Mrs Prance laid down the oars.

'They are such waddlers on land,' she commented. 'But in the sea they are as agile as can be.'

'Keep singing or they'll go away,' Ghillean said. 'They've come to hear your song.'

Once again his mother started to sing, leaving the boat to drift in the sparkling waters.

Fear a' bhàta na hòro èile
Mo shoraidh slàn dhuit's gach
Àit' an teid thu!

Suddenly there was only one seal near the boat. The other one had felt the need to dive for a snack.

'Where's he gone?' asked the lad.

'I don't know,' laughed his mother. 'But he'll have to come up for air soon.'

As though she was determined to join in the fun of the day, the seal swam under the boat and broke water on the other side.

'There she is!' Ghillean said. 'She's playing tricks on us.'

Just along the shore from the jetty was one of the boy's favourite places. There was a shallow shingle beach bordering on the road. And it looked as though an artist had splashed pink, white and yellow all along the roadside.

'Spring is my favourite time of year,' commented Mrs Prance as they reached the shingle. 'The sea pink's flowers are like fairy lollipops.'

'What does the white campion look like?' Ghillean asked.

'I don't know,' laughed his mother. 'What do you think?'

The lad studied the white flowers before deciding they looked like the lacy mats on which his godmother served her home-made scones.

'And the yellow vetch,' said Mrs Prance, 'what do you think it looks like?'

As Ghillean studied the plant closely, his mother smiled at the pleasure her son found in nature.

'I think,' said Ghillean, 'that the flowers look like rabbits' faces with long ears, and the leaves are like zip fasteners...' he paused for effect, 'the curly tendrils look as though they're reaching out to catch me!'

'I think we should be heading back home for tea or Cousin Margaret will be reaching out to catch us both!' concluded his mother.

A year later the Prance family moved from Dunvegan on the Isle of Skye in Scotland to a lovely house surrounded by 50 acres of woodland in the English county of Gloucestershire. Ghillean and his sisters were happy there to start with. There was plenty of exploring to be done, trees to be climbed, and hide and seek just asking to be played. But their joy in their new surroundings was not to last. Mr Prance died in 1946, when Ghillean was just nine years old. His young heart was broken. When he felt a need to be alone, he took himself into the woodland and looked at the trees, birds, flowers and insects. It was easier for the boy to look outside of himself than to look into his sad heart.

'What are you doing today?' Mrs Prance asked some time later.

'I'm going to read my favourite book,' said Ghillean.

'Now, I wonder what that will be,' his mother smiled. 'May I guess?'

Her son grinned. He knew that she would never guess the amazing book he had discovered.

'Is it *Uncle Tom's Cabin*?'

Ghillean shook his head.

'Is it *Kidnapped*?'

'I knew you would never guess,' Ghillean laughed aloud. 'My favourite book is *Gilbert White's Natural History of Selborne*.'

Mrs Prance looked puzzled. 'I know the one,' she said. 'It's an old book that's been in the house as long as I can remember. Tell me about it.'

Ghillean ran to fetch the book, raced back to the sitting room where his mother had made herself comfortable on the settee, and crash-landed beside her.

'I take it you really do like this book when you are so keen to show me it,' Mum laughed.

Turning the pages slowly one by one, Ghillean showed his mother picture after picture of plants and birds, trees and insects.

'You see, Mum,' the boy said, 'this book is full of things I know about. The trees in our wood are here. There are drawings of the wild flowers, and descriptions of the birds too. When I found a beetle I'd not seen before I looked it up and discovered what kind it was.'

Mrs Prance watched her son's enthusiasm and realised that he was expert beyond his years in the study of nature.

'Nature study is a lovely hobby,' she said. 'It's a hobby you'll be able to continue with whatever you do for a living.'

By the time Ghillean went to boarding school, aged twelve, his particular interest was in wild flowers. And, much to his surprise and delight, one of his masters was every bit as keen as he was. Mr Bill Wilson was so keen on botany (the study of plants) that he spent weekends, even some holidays, taking pupils on trips to find rare plants. Not only that, but Ghillean had several aunts, two of whom were keen botanists who did all they could to encourage the boy in his interest. They also began to teach him about plant families, and they called plants by their Latin names rather than their English ones.

'How many names can one plant have?' the lad laughed, when he and his aunts were looking though a book together. 'Up in Dunvegan we called that plant sea pink, though I knew it was also called thrift. Now I've discovered that its botanical name is *Armeria maritimae.*'

As Ghillean climbed through his teenage years his interest in plants became more than just a hobby. And, by the time he had to decide what to study at university, there was no decision to be taken. Ghillean Prance would go to Oxford and study botany.

'Would you like to come to a tea for new students?' a member of the Christian Union asked, within a few days of the beginning of term.

'Yes, thanks,' Ghillean answered.

The student who invited him seemed a nice sort, and going to university is a good time to make new friends and discover interesting new things. Another invitation followed soon afterwards.

'Would you like to come to church next Sunday evening?'

Once again, Ghillean accepted. And at that Sunday service he heard a sermon like none he'd ever heard before. Three weeks later the first year botany student became a Christian. Jesus was his Saviour and Friend.

Botany took on a whole new meaning. Not only was Ghillean learning new and wonderful things about plants, he was discovering more and more about the great Creator God who made every one of them. The young botanist looked with wonder through his microscope at the amazing detail God put into even the most insignificant of plants. Not only did Ghillean study botany, he also studied his Bible. To his delight, his two studies came together as he read verses like: 'Come and see what God has done, how awesome his works on man's behalf!' It seemed to him, as he looked at plants under the microscope, that he was discovering awesome works of creation, all made by God to benefit and delight mankind.

In July 1961, Ghillean married Anne, whom he had met at a beach mission a few months after he became a Christian. Several exciting field trips later, the Prances moved from England to America, where he began work with the New York Botanical Garden. Although he was based in New York, much of his time was spent on plant-hunting expeditions in the Amazon Basin, in Brazil.

'Even if we have to watch every penny we spend,' Anne said, after she'd been left alone in New York with their two daughters, while he was away on an expedition, 'we must go back as a family. It's lonely being left behind.'

That was why the Prance family moved to South America and made their home in Brazil.

'I've been asked to assist in the Amazonian Research Institute,' Ghillean explained some time later.

'What will that involve?' asked Anne.

'We're to set up a university course in Amazonian botany for Brazilian students.'

Anne didn't need to ask if her husband would like to do that ... Of course he would.

Ghillean invited one of his colleagues from New York to come and lecture to the students on ecology, the science of looking after the earth and all that lives and grows.

'I think we should take the students to see the Trans-Amazon Highway,' one of the men suggested.

That was agreed but no one could have guessed the outcome. The Trans-Amazon Highway cut through hundreds of miles of rainforest ... and left utter devastation. Ghillean, Robert Goodland, and the students could hardly believe what they were seeing.

On their return, the two men wrote articles about what was happening, and they made such a fuss that people began to listen to what they were saying.

'What does it matter if a few miles of trees are hacked down?' some said.

But if they said it to Ghillean Prance, he told them exactly why it mattered. Land treated in that terrible way could never be the same again. People, animals, birds, trees, plants and insects, all were badly affected by the disastrous road project.

'And the thing is,' he would say, 'the plan to build villages along the highway for settlers from other parts of Brazil isn't even working. They don't know how to live there.'

The Indian peoples were of great interest to Ghillean Prance. And if anyone suggested that they were 'primitive', he was quick to correct them.

'I've learned more from my Indian friends about plants than from any of my Oxford University professors,' he insisted. 'They understand and care for the natural world in a way that we don't. And they treat it with

57

a respect that planners and developers have long forgotten.'

In his years working in the Amazon Basin, Ghillean worked along with fourteen different tribes of Amazonian Indians, making good friends among them and learning new things from them.

In 1987, the Director of Kew Gardens near London retired. The Royal Botanic Gardens, Kew, are the best-known gardens in the whole world.

'Would you consider applying for the job?' six different people asked Ghillean, all in the space of seven days!

He did apply. But a week before he flew to England for his interview a hurricane hit Kew, a hurricane so severe that it destroyed over a thousand trees. Ghillean wondered if there was anything left of the great gardens at all. There was. Although 1,000 trees came down, over 9,000 still stood tall and strong. The interview went well, and Ghillean Prance became Director of the Royal Botanic Gardens. The Prance family said goodbye to Brazil, to New York, and headed east across the Atlantic Ocean to England.

'Does that remind you of Brazil?' someone asked Anne one day, as they stood beside the giant water lily *Victoria amazonica* in Kew.

Anne smiled. 'Yes, it does. And let me tell

you about it. My husband would spend all night in revolting, smelly, still waters studying the lily, and in the mornings he brought me two things. One was a disgusting bag of smelly clothes to be washed, and the other was a sack of water lily flowers. I had to cut each in half and count the number of beetles I found there.'

'I didn't know you were interested in insects,' her companion laughed.

'I'm not. But I did become something of an expert beetle-catcher!'

'Could you sum up your personal vision for Kew in just a few words?' asked a journalist, who was writing an article about the new Director.

'Yes,' said Ghillean. 'I think I can. My vision for the Royal Botanic Gardens, Kew, is that they lead the world in thinking about conservation. We are facing a most serious environmental crisis, and we must do all in our power to prevent it. The earth belongs to the Lord; he made it. Our job is to look after it for him.'

The journalist glanced up from his notes.

'Do you really believe God made the earth?' he asked.

Ghillean smiled. 'I do,' he said. 'I most certainly do.'

Fact File: The Amazon
The Amazon rain forests are being destroyed at near record levels. 26,000 square kilometres of forest were chopped down in the twelve months prior to August 2004. The figure is the second highest on record, 6% higher than the previous twelve months. Deforestation was worst in the state of Mato Grosso where vast swathes of land have been cleared to grow crops. The loss of 26,000 square kilometres means almost a fifth of the entire Amazon has now been cleared.

Keynote: It is important to remember that God has given us his creation to look after and not to squander and destroy. He has given us resources to use and make use of but these are not to be used without thought or used in a selfish and greedy way. In the book of Genesis Adam and Eve are given the task of looking after the Garden of Eden. It is sad to see how sin has indeed destroyed so much of God's creation. The destructive effect that humanity has had on the land and living creatures is just one part of that.

Think: Can you think of some ways that you can look after the plants and animals in your world? You can feed birds in the winter months and help keep your environment clean by tidying away rubbish in bins. But you should also consider recycling. Try and reuse paper and then put it into a recycling bin. Do you leave the tap running when you brush your teeth? Do you leave the lights on in the house when you don't need to? These are just little things but they all contribute towards helping to look after the world that God has given us.

 Prayer: Dear Lord, thank you for the world that you have given us. Thank you for water and food that we need for daily life. Thank you for the colours and the beauty that we see all around us. We know that you care for your creation, as your Word tells us that not even a sparrow falls to the ground without your knowledge. Your love for sinners meant that you sent your son to die for them on the cross. We thank you for that and ask that you will help us to tell others about you and about your love for people and the world.

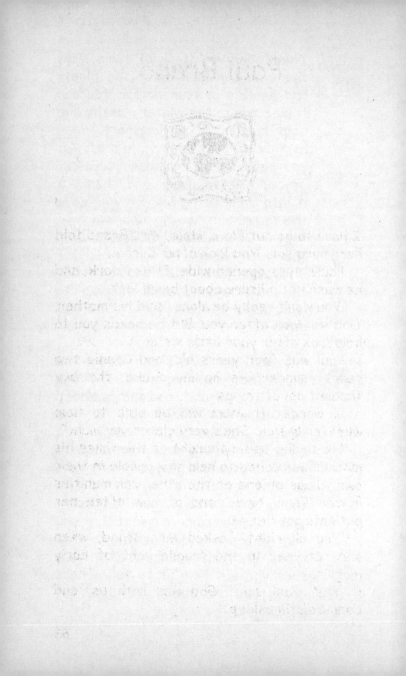

Paul Brand

'I have to go out for a while,' Mrs Brand told her young son. 'You look after Connie.'

Paul's eyes opened wide. It was dark, and he wasn't at all sure about being left.

'You won't really be alone,' said his mother. 'God will look after you. But he needs you to help look after your little sister.'

Paul was four years old, and Connie two years younger. As he lay awake, the boy thought about things.

'I wonder if Mum will be able to help whoever is sick. She's very clever, my mum.'

He smiled as he thought of the times his mother was called to help sick people in their own village or one of the other communities in the Tamil Nadu, and of how often her patients got better.

'You all right?' asked Mrs Brand, when she returned in the fragile light of early morning.

'Yes,' Paul said. 'God was with us, and Connie's still asleep.'

'Mum, are you a real doctor?' Paul asked the following morning, as she cleaned a cut on his knee.

Mrs Brand smiled. 'No,' she explained. 'I'm not a real doctor. I've not done full medical training. But the people I treat are real patients. God kindly allows me to help them.'

'Is Dad a real doctor?'

Mrs Brand smiled. 'I'm sorry to disappoint you,' she said. 'Dad's not a real doctor either. Come, let me explain.'

Sitting outside their little home on stilts in the village of Kolli Malai, high in the mountains of South West India, Mrs Brand told her children how it came about that they were growing up there.

'Dad and I both felt that God was leading us to come here to serve the people and to tell them about the Lord Jesus Christ. That's why we left England for India. And in order to be of help to the people here, both of us did a course in tropical medicine. You see, many of the diseases here are different from those in England, which means that our training in tropical medicine was very helpful. But, of course, there are things that we don't know about that real doctors understand.'

Paul, a very intelligent little boy, was full of questions.

'What diseases do people in England not have that we have here?'

'Well,' his mum said, 'they don't have bubonic plague, black water fever or malaria. Cholera is very rare in England now, though it was a real problem till the end of last century.'

'What about influenza?' the child asked, remembering what had happened a few months before in a village near Kolli Malai.

'Yes, they do have influenza, and sometimes people die of it.'

Mrs Brand's face looked suddenly sad. 'Do you remember when influenza hit the mountain village above us last year?'

Paul nodded.

'Every single person in the village died,' she said. 'Not one survived. Back in Britain, when influenza strikes some people die, but never a whole town or village.'

'Why does it happen here then?' the lad asked.

'I suppose it's mainly because the people here are poor and underfed and not really strong enough to fight against diseases.'

Paul smiled, much to his mother's surprise, as it seemed a sad topic to smile about.

'I think you know just as much as a real doctor,' he said. 'And I think Dad does too.'

It was ten days later, and there was great excitement in the village of Kolli Malai, especially in the Brand home.

'Dad should be home today,' Paul told his sister.

The very word 'Dad' made the little girl smile. She saw him first. 'Dad! Dad!' she yelled in the local language.

Mr Brand was no sooner home than people crowded round to see him, including a man who had just arrived in the village with a bundle of rags. Pushing past the local villagers, the man handed the bundle to the missionary. It was Connie who first yelled 'Baby', for it was she who noticed the tiny hand sticking out of the bundle.

'What do we have here?' asked Mr Brand gently.

He was told that the baby's mother was ill and that it seemed the baby was dying.

The baby was undressed from its hot wrappings, then washed and had his poor sticky eyes cleaned. He was fed tiny drops of boiled cooled water and wiped with a clean damp cloth over and over again to bring down his temperature.

'Look Dad,' said Paul, who was most interested in what was going on. 'The baby's eyes are opening. Can I do anything to help him?'

'Yes, you can,' said Mr Brand. 'You can do two things. You can sit beside him and pray for him – with your eyes open – because I want you to tell me if he sicks up any of that water.'

Paul did exactly as he was told. The lad would have been very surprised if anyone had told him so, but that afternoon he was doing exactly what his parents went to India to do – he was caring for the bodies and the souls of the people of the Tamil Nadu.

The Brand children were a year or two older when they saw something that remained with Paul for the rest of his life. Three strangers came slowly up the mountain one day looking for Mr Brand. The missionary always welcomed people whoever they were but Paul was aware that these people received a different kind of welcome from usual.

'What's Dad doing?' the boy wondered, as he watched.

Then he screwed up his face. The three strangers had white patches on their dark skin, and it looked as though the ends of their fingers had fallen off.

'Look at their feet!' he exclaimed. 'No wonder they can't walk properly.'

The men had hardly any toes at all.

Paul watched, fascinated by the horror of what he was seeing and at his father's unusual response.

'Why's Dad putting on gloves?' he wondered.

Mr Brand took a basin of water and washed the poor deformed feet, then rubbed ointment on to them. At one and the same time his son tried to see what was going on and tried not to look because it wasn't very nice at all.

'Here comes Mum to give them a basket of food,' Paul told Connie. 'But she can't like the look of them either because she's not going near.'

Having had their feet dressed in strips of cloth the men hobbled off, taking the food with them.

'I'll go and take the basket to Mum,' said Paul, trying to be helpful.

'No!' Mrs Brand's voice rang out, when she saw what he was about to do. 'Don't touch that!'

The boy felt confused at his mother's response, and very much more confused when he saw her lifting the basket with a stick and putting it on the fire to burn! Meanwhile, Mr Brand scrubbed his hands in hot water and with strong soap, took off his clothes, scrubbed again then dressed in clean clothes. Only after all of that were Mr and Mrs Brand able to relax and explain what the problem was.

'These men have leprosy,' Mr Brand told the children.

Paul shivered. He'd read about people with leprosy in the Bible, and knew that no one went near them apart from Jesus who made some of them better. That night, as he lay in bed with his mosquito net tucked firmly under his mattress, he thought of his parents, and of how kind and brave they were as they tried to be like Jesus.

Not long after that the family went home to England for a while. Paul and Connie remained there to go to school when their parents went back to India. Every day Mr and Mrs Brand wrote part of a letter to their children. When it was long enough they posted it to the two young folk they loved most in the world. Sadly, in 1929, Mr Brand died before his children could see him again. He died of black water fever, one of the diseases that exist in India but not in Britain.

When Paul left school he didn't think he wanted to be a doctor but some years later God showed him that that was exactly what he should do with his life. By 1940 the Second World War was raging and Paul had plenty to keep him busy.

'There's been a huge bombing raid tonight,' he was told. 'Everyone to Accident and Emergency.'

'What damage glass can do,' Paul thought, as he picked tiny shards out of a little boy's face and arms. Then he began work on his hands.

'Poor lad,' he said, 'he's obviously put his hands up to shield his face. Look at the mess they're in.'

It took ages to pick the glass out of the lad's hands, and that gave Paul time to think.

'You know,' he told a friend afterwards, 'hands are absolutely beautifully made.'

Paul Brand married Margaret in 1943 and God led them to live in India and to bring up their family there. He also used Paul's previous experiences to do very wonderful things. Having seen leprosy as a boy, he now saw it through the eyes of a very fine surgeon.

'What's your name and what age are you?' Paul asked a new patient who came to his clinic in 1951.

'Sadagopan,' the boy said. 'And I'm eight.'

'Tell me what's happened to you.'

'I can't feel anything with my fingers,' said Sadagopan. 'And I have white patches on my body and ulcers on my feet.'

'Are they sore?'

'No,' the lad said. 'I couldn't walk on them if they were sore.'

'How did you get here?' Paul asked.

'I was told you could help me so I walked for days to get here.'

The doctor looked at Sadagopan's feet and could see the terrible damage that walking to the hospital in Vellore had caused.

Paul Brand put an arm around the boy and took held his damaged hands. Sadagopan was shocked and speechless. The doctor had touched him! That night the weary boy slept peacefully, smiling occasionally in his sleep.

'Sadagopan,' Paul said. 'I want to explain what I can do for you.'

The lad, who by then loved Dr Brand very much indeed, listened carefully.

'I'll put you to sleep, then operate on your hands. I can cut them open with special instruments and work right inside them.'

'That won't make them better,' said Sadagopan quietly, 'it will be very sore.'

'I think I can help you to use what's left of your hands,' said Paul. 'And I think I can help you to prevent more damage to your feet.'

The boy looked utterly disbelieving.

'And you won't feel anything at all during the operation, but there will be times when you'll be sore as you get better. You would have to be very courageous.'

Sadagopan, brave boy that he was, agreed to let Paul do what he could for him.

The surgeon operated several times on his patient's damaged hands and was able to give him useful movement again. Paul also had special shoes made for Sadagopan. They didn't rub and cause more damage, and helped the boy to walk without hurting his feet.

'Look at Sadagopan,' a nurse said some months after he'd arrived at Vellore Christian Hospital. 'He looks a different boy.'

'In what way?' asked a stranger, who'd not seen the lad before.

The nurse explained. 'When Sadagopan came here the only life he could expect was that of a beggar, and he knew it. He was just a sad scrap of humanity.'

'Really?' gasped the stranger, looking at the boy weaving a basket and laughing at a joke as he wove.

Sadagopan was just one boy whose life was completely changed by what Dr Brand was able to do for him. To Sadagopan it seemed like a miracle, and that is how very many people have felt in the years since Paul began his pioneering surgery.

'When I think back to Dad's treatment of leprosy,' Paul told a friend one day, 'I realise how much things have changed. Then nothing could be done apart from applying cream to the ulcers. And people were scared to do even that in case they caught the disease themselves. At least Dad did what he could.'

'So what made the difference?' his friend asked.

'I suppose it was the realisation that it wasn't the disease that damaged hands and feet but that people did it themselves because the disease made them lose feeling. As they didn't feel pain they could stand on burning embers, or a snake, and not feel the injury. And because they didn't feel the injury, they didn't know to treat it and their situation just went from bad to worse.'

What Paul Brand didn't tell his friend was that it was he who convinced doctors that was the case.

'You see,' Paul said, 'God designed the human body so that it is able to survive because of pain. Pain is the body's warning system to tell us that something is wrong and we should do something about it.'

Margaret Brand, who was also a medical missionary, worked on the prevention of blindness in those who suffered from leprosy. After doing over 3,000 operations in the hospital at Vellore, Paul and Margaret moved to America in 1966, where he worked on rehabilitation. Rehabilitation is helping people to make the very best of anything they are able to do: helping ill or injured people to walk, to use their hands, to work ... to live.

In the summer of 2003, Dr Paul Brand died and went to heaven. There he was welcomed by Jesus, who himself reached out and touched and healed those suffering from leprosy.

Fact File: Leprosy
Leprosy is a medical condition, also known as Hansen's Disease, after Armauer Hansen, a Norwegian doctor who was the first to view the leprosy microbe under a microscope in 1873. It is neither hereditary nor flesh eating. Many think that it is a disease of the past but leprosy still affects hundreds of thousands of people around the world. Most leprosy cases arise in Asia, South America and Africa. Last year over 500,000 new cases were detected - that's over 1,400 people every day.

Keynote: There are many diseases and illnesses that are difficult to cure and there are still many that are incurable. When Jesus was on this earth leprosy was an incurable disease and people didn't know anything about it. If you had the disease you were forced to leave home and people wouldn't even come near you. But one day Jesus healed ten lepers from their disease. Can you imagine how these men must have felt? But only one of them came back to thank him. Make sure that you follow that man's example and thank God for your health.

Think: Even when we are sick God is still with us. We can pray for a cure but this may not be something that we will receive. God's answers to our prayers can be 'Yes', 'No' or 'Wait'. When we are suffering we can pray to God to help us. He can give us the strength to carry on – even though we are ill, even though we may never get better.

Prayer: Lord Jesus, thank you for your love and mercy. Thank you for how you showed this love to all people – sick and healthy. Help us to show your love to others. Help us to be loving and caring to people in hospital and old folk's homes. Help us to be welcoming to boys and girls from other countries and to show friendship to people who are lonely and afraid.

Johann Sebastian Bach

'Let's play hide and seek,' said Johann Sebastian to a friend. 'This house is great for it!'

So, while Johann ran to hide, the young boy began the long count to fifty.

'Will I hide in the grain store or in one of the students' rooms?' wondered Johann Sebastian. 'No, I know, I'll hide in Dad's music room.'

Tiptoeing along the corridor, Johann reached the music room and crept in. Looking around, he made up his mind where to hide.

'I'll lie down here behind the harpsichord. And if I pull this rug over myself and put Dad's trumpet on top, he'll never find me.'

'Forty-nine, fifty!' yelled Johann's friend. 'And here I come!'

Footsteps were heard running upstairs to where the students lived, downstairs to the grain store and along to the sunny room in which the family played music together. But Johann could not be found anywhere.

'He wouldn't dare go into his father's music room,' thought the boy. 'He'd be skinned alive if he damaged anything there.'

But, having failed to find his friend, the boy opened the music room door and waited – a little scared to go in.

'Aaaa….tishshoo!' exploded from under the rug behind the harpsichord. And as it did, a trumpet crashed to the ground.

'Caught you!' yelled the boy. 'But, I'm off before your dad comes to see what the noise is.'

Music was everywhere in the Bach home, in the German town of Eisenach. Herr Bach, Johann Sebastian's father, was court trumpeter to the Duke of Eisenach, and he taught music students. Some even stayed in their home. The Bach family were famous for music. Johann Sebastian, who was only seven years old, already had his own little violin, and he was learning to play the harpsichord.

'Your uncle would like to teach you to play the organ too,' Herr Bach said, when his son had finished his violin practice. 'Would you like that?'

The boy thought of the magnificent music his uncle played in the St Georgenkirche in Eisenach, and said 'yes' right away.

'I'm starting at the Latin Grammar School next term,' Johann Sebastian told his friend the following year, 1693.

'You'll only study the Bible there,' the lad laughed. 'They are so proud that Martin Luther used to be a pupil they're not interested in anything else.'

Everyone in Eisenach knew about Martin Luther. In the early 16th Century he had studied the Bible and discovered that the church was teaching very wrong things. He'd also taught Bible truths in a day when people were burned at the stake for doing so. Luther was not martyred for his faith but the Pope had many of his books burned as a warning to others. That period of church history is called the Reformation, and Martin Luther was one of the most famous Reformers.

'Of course they study other things,' laughed Johann. 'We study Latin at least, because it's called the Latin Grammar School.'

The boys from the school made up the choir of the St Georgenkirche and before long Johann was a member.

'The music makes my skin tingle,' he thought. 'God must enjoy listening to it.'

Johann's skin tingled especially when he sang solo. As the notes soared higher he felt he was reaching up to God himself.

'Have you heard the news?' the boys at school asked each other just a few months later. 'Johann Sebastian's mother has died.'

'Imagine losing your mother when you're nine,' one friend said sadly. 'Who would look after you?'

'I suppose Herr Bach will look after him, and his servants will always be there to help,' someone answered. 'But it must be horrible.'

Before a year had passed the same group of boys were standing outside the school before classes began.

'It's terrible news about Johann's father dying. I wonder what will happen to him now.'

'That means he's an orphan. But I suppose he'll go to stay with one of his big brothers.'

'We'll miss him. But I won't miss the arguments we have. The annoying thing is that most of the arguments are about music, and he's usually right!'

Johann Sebastian went to live with his brother, Johann Christoph, and his wife in Ohrdruf. There were 14 years between Johann and his older brother.

'I'm glad you're able to teach me music,' the young boy told his brother. 'You're a great teacher.'

'The Bachs are all great teachers,' Johann Christoph smiled. 'And they are all great pupils, you included. I hope you'll be as good a pupil at your new school.'

The boy did work hard at the Ohrdruf grammar school, studying theology, Latin and Greek. Of course, much of Johann Sebastian's time was taken up with his music.

'It's very good for young musicians to copy what the old masters wrote,' Johann

Christoph told his brother. 'For tomorrow I'd like you to copy out this page by Jakob Froberger. Do it so carefully that you'll be able to play from it.'

Copying music became rather a hobby for Johann Sebastian, because he could hear the music in his head as he wrote.

'May I copy this piece?' he asked one day. 'It's new music, and I really like it.'

'No,' his brother said firmly. 'I want you to stick to the old masters.'

But Johann really did like that piece of modern music. So he went to the music room late at night and copied it by moonlight. It took him six whole months. Was his brother pleased with his enthusiasm? He most certainly was not!

'I like Martin Luther's hymns' said Johann Sebastian. 'He says what I believe. The words make me want to write music for them.'

'Do that then,' he was told. 'See if you can write music to fit these words, though Martin Luther wrote his own tune for this hymn.'

The boy read the words aloud.

Glory to God in highest heaven,
Who unto man his Son has given!
While angels sing with pious mirth
A glad New Year to all the earth.'

Sitting at the organ he played Luther's tune, then made an arrangement of his own.

81

Before he laid his pen down, Johann Sebastian wrote across the bottom of the manuscript paper the words, 'To the glory of God.' Young though he was, he wanted his music to praise his Lord in heaven.

'Are you serious?' a friend asked one day, when Johann suggested that they walk to Lüneburg to hear the great organist Dietrich Buxtehude. 'Do you know how far that is?'

'It's a mere eighty miles or so,' laughed Johann Sebastian.

'And a mere eighty miles or so back, making it a mere 160 miles round trip!' his friend said. 'That's serious walking.'

The pair of them did go, and all to hear someone play the organ wonderfully well. Bach was just fifteen years old at the time.

Over the years that followed the young man worked as a professional musician in various parts of his homeland. Bach lived in Lüneburg and then in Weimar before moving on to Arnstadt in 1703, where he began to focus on the organ.

'The Arnstadt organ is splendid,' he wrote to one of his brothers. 'It has two manuals and twenty-three speaking stops. And I love being responsible for the congregation's music.'

Three years later, his letters were less enthusiastic. 'The choirboys are awful! They shuffle about and don't learn their parts. One even spoke back to me the other day. And, would you believe it, some of the people in the congregation don't like my musical arrangements. They say they are "too ornamental!" The truth is that they just don't want to understand them.'

Not surprisingly, Johann Sebastian applied for another job and moved to Mühlhausen in 1707. While he was there he married another Bach, his cousin Maria Barbara. In those days professional musicians moved from place to place. They sometimes served as church musicians or worked for grand families who had their own musicians. Once an employer put Bach in prison for a month to prevent him moving to another job. For five years Johann Sebastian worked for Prince Leopold of Anhalt-Cöthen, who had an orchestra of eighteen players. Bach was his Capellmeister*, the highest rank of musician at that time.

'I can't take it in,' Johann Sebastian said in a trembling voice. 'When I went away with the Prince and the orchestra, I left behind a dear wife and a happy family. Now you're telling me that Maria Barbara is dead, that my children are motherless.'

He sat down heavily. It was as though the last forty-three years had rolled away and he had once again just lost his mother. He knew exactly how his children felt.

*Capellmeister: The director of an orchestra or choir, formerly belonging to a German prince.

'Come,' he said to them later that evening, 'let's make music together.'

The family took their instruments, as they had done so often in the past, and played music that allowed them to feel all the sadness of those who had lost someone they loved.

'Your mother is with the Lord,' Johann Sebastian told his children. 'She is with Jesus, where she will be happier than ever.'

'But she was happy here,' said his youngest son.

Bach smiled at his memories. 'Yes,' he said. 'She was. We had a very happy family life.'

There were to be happy days again in the future for Johann Sebastian married again, and their new stepmother, Anna Magdalena, brought laughter back into their lives.

'Tell us about Leipzig,' Bach's children asked, before they moved there.

'Well, it's the second most important city in Saxony, with about 30,000 people living there. It's a very beautiful city and very forward-thinking. You'll never guess what you'll see there?'

No one could guess.

'The streets of Leipzig are lit up at nights,' their father told them. 'And another wonder in Leipzig is the great new library that has just opened.'

'I think street lights are more wonderful than that,' his daughter laughed.

At the end of May 1723, a North German newspaper carried an interesting account of the Bachs' removal. 'Last Saturday at noon, four carts laden with goods and chattels belonging to the former Capellmeister to the Court of Cöthen arrived in Leipzig and, at two in the afternoon, he and his family arrived in two coaches and moved into their newly decorated lodgings in the school building.' The family that travelled in those coaches were Johann Sebastian, his wife, and four children, aged 8, 9, 12 and 14. The great musician and composer's new job was as Director of Choir and Music in Leipzig.

'What a huge amount of music the Director has written,' one choirboy said. 'Most of it from the Bible.'

'I know,' his friend agreed. 'I was studying the Bible for school the other day, and when I turned the page I realised I knew it already because I'd sung it in one of his cantatas.'

'That's a nice easy way of doing your homework,' Johann Sebastian laughed.

'I'm sorry, Sir,' the boy blushed. 'I didn't know you were there.'

The Director of Music smiled at his pupil. 'Don't worry. It's my hope and prayer that my music leads people to think about the Lord. Although it never occurred to me that it could help you young scamps with your homework.'

That afternoon, as Bach completed work on a new piece of music, he stopped before putting his pen down. Then he wrote at the bottom, 'This work is written to the glory of Almighty God.'

'It's not always easy finding boys to sing in the four churches here in Leipzig,' he said to his wife that evening, after he told her the homework story. 'I have fifty-four boys to choose from. Of them seventeen are good, twenty are getting there, and the other seventeen can't sing the music.'

'But remember they're learning about the Lord as they practise,' Anna Magdalena said.

'True. I'll try to remember that especially when I'm working with the seventeen who can't sing the music. Perhaps that will help me to be more patient with them.'

'I'm really tired,' said Johann Sebastian in 1747. 'It's a privilege to be invited to play for King Fredrick the Great of Prussia, but I think I'm getting too old for travelling.'

'The concert will begin soon,' he was told when he arrived. 'You are just in time.'

'Your visitor is here, your Majesty,' announced a courtier.

The king's eyes lit up. 'Old Bach is here,' he said.

The concert was cancelled, and King Fredrick and the great composer spent the evening together. The king was especially delighted because Johann Sebastian composed a fugue based on a simple tune Fredrick himself had written.

'Blindness is a great trial,' Bach said, less than two years later. 'And the two operations haven't helped at all.'

'If you tell me what to write, I'll take down your music. You can still play it because you know it in your head and heart. It just needs to be written down for other people,' Anna Magdalena said.

It was to his wife that he dictated the notes of his very last composition, a piece of choir music with title, 'Before thy throne I now appear.'

Shortly afterwards the great Johann Sebastian Bach, aged 65, died and appeared before the throne of his God in heaven.

Fact: The Reformation
Bach's ancestors showed a great loyalty to the Reformation and to the teachings of Martin Luther. At some point prior to 1597, a baker named Veit Bach left Hungary for Germany. This was in order to protect his Protestant faith against the increasing persecution in Hungary. Veit established himself once again as a baker, and, from then on future generations of the Bach family became great musicians, the greatest, of course, being Johann Sebastian Bach.

Key note: The Bible today is written in many different languages but originally it was written in Hebrew and Greek. If you look at a copy of a Latin Bible, Romans 16:27 and Jude 25 have the words 'Soli Deo Gloria'— 'to the only God be glory.' This was to become Bach's motto. He would sign all his works with the initials SDG. It didn't matter if they were deep theological works or light-hearted ones – they were all written to the glory of God.

Think: Is there a difference between doing work in a church and doing work somewhere such as a hospital, shop or sports hall? Is one job better than another? Is one job holier and more virtuous than the other? In the Bible God tells us that we are to do everything as if we were doing it for God. And we are to do it with all our might.

 Prayer: Thank you, Lord, for work and employment. Thank you for learning, teachers and books. Help me to appreciate the gift of education when so many children do not have it. Help me to do all that I can for your glory. You are the one who gives me strength and intelligence. I thank you for providing for me in so many ways. Help me to trust in you even when it seems that life is a struggle, times are hard and money scarce.

Samuel Morse

At four years old Samuel Morse was already at school. Usually when school ended for the afternoon he raced home and forgot all about it, but not today.

'Did you have a good day at school?' his father asked.

Papa was a minister in Charlestown, Massachusetts, and he was very interested in his son's education.

Samuel held his head low.

'Something wrong?' Papa asked.

The boy nodded his head.

'Do you want to come into my study to talk?'

His father's study was where serious things were talked about. Samuel thought for a minute and then went with his Papa into the study. Jedidiah Morse sat down on one side of the fire and told his son to sit on the other. Samuel perched himself on the edge of his chair and swung his legs, for they didn't quite reach the ground.

'Tell me about it,' said Papa, then he sat and waited till his young son was ready to talk.

'On my way to school this morning I found a pin on the road,' Samuel began, looking straight in his father's eyes. He had been taught to be open and truthful. 'I pinned it on my shirt to play with later. Then, when Old Ma'am Rand was working with the other boys, I remembered about the pin. I was so bored.'

Mr Morse would normally have reminded Samuel not to call his teacher old, and that clever children should never be bored ... but he let it go. There was obviously something else coming.

'As she wasn't watching me, I decided to do a drawing of her ... on the chest of drawers ... with my pin. It was a very good drawing, very like her.'

'Go on,' said Papa, seriously.

'You know Ma'am Rand is disabled, and can't chase us. Well, when she saw me she told me to go to her desk. I thought she was going to beat me with the cane. But ....'

'But what?' Papa asked, after a long silence.

Samuel looked into his father's eyes once more.

'She pinned me to her dress so that I would have to stay there right beside her all day. I couldn't do that, Papa,' he said, his eyes beginning to fill with tears. 'So I pulled myself away … and it only made a little rip in her dress. She laid out at me with her cane and hit me here,' he concluded, rubbing his shoulder.

There was some serious talking done in the study that afternoon, and some praying, before Samuel Morse and his father went to join the rest of the family for dinner.

It was the year 1795, and Samuel Morse paid the price of being a talented artist.

Samuel was thirteen years old when he decided to keep a diary.

'What will I write in it?' he wondered. 'I want it to be special.'

The teenager spent some time thinking about it and then made a list of things he would record.

'I'll write about what happens at home and school, local news, the books I read and the weather. I'll put some drawings in too. Then, when I'm old, I'll read it and see how much I remember about being young. Perhaps one day I'll have a son and he can read it too and discover what his father was like as a boy.'

As he sat back and wondered how to begin, he laughed out loud.

'I'd better watch my spelling,' he said to himself. 'When I was at Phillips Academy in Andover my school report gave me five bad marks for spelling … and another eighteen for whispering. At least I can't spoil my nice new diary by whispering to it.'

The three Morse boys had a happy childhood in a fine Christian home. They had freedom to play wild and adventurous games, though they had to do their lessons first. But there was sadness too. Over the years a further seven children were born, either dead or so sickly that they died as young babies.

'I now write to you again to inform you that Mama had a baby, but it was born dead and has just been buried,' Samuel wrote to his brothers. 'You now have three brothers and three sisters in heaven and I hope you and I will meet them there at our death.'

Samuel knew a great deal about life and death, even though he was just fourteen years old, and he trusted in the Lord Jesus that he would go to heaven when he died.

'Why must I go to Yale College?' Samuel asked his father. 'That's not where my friends are going.'

'I know,' Mr Morse agreed. 'But you'll get the best education. What's taught there is based on the best book of all, the Bible.'

'Then it must be good,' the boy agreed. 'And I suppose I'll make new friends when I get there.'

Samuel was still fourteen when he began

his studies at Yale College, and he did make friends very quickly, even with some of the members of staff.

'Science is fascinating' Samuel wrote to a friend in Charlestown. 'My professor says that Christians should not be afraid of studying science as they are studying God's wonderful world. When I see you, I'll tell you what happened in science class the other day.'

When they did meet, Samuel's friend could hardly believe what he heard.

'Professor Day made us stand in a circle holding hands,' the boy remembered. 'The idea was that an electrical current would pass round the circle, going right through each one of us.'

His friend's eyebrows rose.

'Well, he joined us up to a generator ... and switched it on. Immediately, every one of us left the ground amid cries and screams that could be heard all though the College! We were pretty shaken when Professor Day switched off the generator. I don't know what we were meant to learn from the experiment, but I learned something I'll never forget.'

'What's that?' asked his friend.

Samuel laughed. 'Electricity is a powerful force ... for it forced us all off the ground!'

'Papa, I know you don't think I'm good enough,' Samuel said, when they were discussing his future, 'but I really do want to be an artist.'

'It's not that I don't think you're good,' admitted Mr Morse. 'You are. You wouldn't be able to sell your portraits if you were not. It's just that I don't think you realise how hard it is to be a successful artist. Many try it, but few succeed. If you had a nice steady job like a bookseller, you could paint in your free time. Art's a wonderful hobby, you know.'

Samuel despaired of convincing his father, but his Heavenly Father understood. The teenager prayed that God would show him what to do with his life. Meanwhile, he did what his father suggested. For a while after leaving Yale he worked as a bookseller, spending most of his free time painting.

'You know,' Mr Morse said to his wife after a while, 'I wonder if we are being fair to Samuel. He's so keen to paint, and he does seem to be very talented.'

'But we can't afford to train him,' his wife objected. 'On your minister's salary it's hard making ends meet as it is.'

'God will open the way if that's what he wants,' the minister said. 'And the more I pray about it, the more I feel that is what he wants the lad to do.'

Mr and Mrs Morse searched for every saving they could make and sent their gifted son to London to study art.

'That's very bad, Sir,' Morse's art teacher said, shaking his head. 'The skin looks the colour of mud.'

Samuel looked at the painting – one he was pleased with - and saw it through his teacher's eyes.

'Here, let me show you,' Mr Allston said.

Wiping part of Morse's palette clean, and using fresh paint, Mr Allston demonstrated to his pupil how to create a good flesh colour. Although Mr Allston rarely paid Samuel a compliment, he taught him a very great deal. His young student became a great artist.

War broke out in 1812. It sometimes took Samuel's letters a long time to reach home.

'I'm glad that we know he's a Christian,' Mrs Morse said, 'for he's safe in God's hands.'

'Yes,' agreed her husband, 'the famous Mr William Wilberforce seems to have made a huge impression on our boy. Parents have no greater joy than knowing that their children are trusting in the Lord Jesus, and that they're among God's people.'

They were quite right. Samuel took his faith seriously. He kept a diary and each day answered these questions: How did I pray? Did I feel weighed down with sin? Did I pray like the self-righteous Pharisee? Have I received blessings for which I've not been thankful?

Three years later Samuel returned to America and married Lucretia Walker, but, after just seven years of marriage, his young wife died. Samuel, who was away painting at the time, did not know about her death for some days. When he returned home it was to discover that his children had no mother.

'I wish there was a way to get a message from one place to another,' he thought sadly. 'It's terrible not to know when your family needs you.'

Samuel was so sad that he nearly gave up painting. He had always been interested in making things, even inventing a machine that could cut three-dimensional marble copies of sculptures. For the middle years of his life Samuel Morse travelled in America and Europe painting, though inventing was never far from his mind.

'I want to paint historical pictures,' he said to himself, 'but the only way I can earn enough money is to paint portraits. Not my favourite subject. Why are people willing to pay to see their own faces on a wall when they can see them perfectly well in a mirror?'

The artist laughed out loud. 'It's just as well they do,' he thought, 'or I'd go hungry.'

In 1832 Samuel Morse was sailing to New York, where he'd been appointed as a professor of painting and sculpture.

'What are these men saying?' he asked, when he overheard a discussion. Moving closer to the men who were talking, he listened. They were having a discussion about electricity.

'Can electricity only be conducted through a short length of wire?' Morse asked, after he'd joined the group.

'No, not at all,' Charles Jackson answered. 'It can pass through any known length of wire.'

'If that's the case,' he said, 'then why can't information be transmitted by electricity.'

That night, as Samuel Morse tried to fall asleep in his cabin on the packet-ship* *Sully*, his mind went back to his young wife's death. 'If the family had been able to get in touch with me I could have been with Lucretia when her dear heart failed.'

From then on, Morse concentrated on inventing the electric telegraph rather than painting. He found someone to fund his research and a congressman to advise him.

'If a message can go ten miles without stopping, I can make it go round the world,' he said, and that's what he set out to do.

'You think a message from that contraption can go round the world?' a visitor laughed.

Morse looked at the first telegraph model. It was made of such odds and ends as an artist's canvas stretcher, the wheels of a wooden clock and a length of carpeting.

* Packet-ship: a ship that regularly carried packets of letters, passengers etc. between ports.

'I do,' Samuel said, 'or one based on the same idea.'

In September 1837, an updated model transmitted a message in code through 1,700 feet of wire running back and forward across a room.

'It's the beginning,' Samuel said. 'One day it will cross the world.'

At first each letter of the alphabet was represented by a number. The person receiving a message had to count the number of taps to decide what letter was being relayed.

'There must be an simpler way than that,' Samuel thought, his notebook in his hand, as usual.

Scribbling possible codes, one after the other, he sat back and looked at the sheet.

'Dots and dashes,' he said. 'That would work. Each letter could have a simple combination of dots and dashes, and that could be passed along as short and long bursts of electricity in the telegraph. Now, how do I work out the code? The most common letters should have the shortest codes, and the least common should have longer ones. Each number could have a dot/dash code too!'

On 24th May 1844, after many ups and downs (mostly downs for financial reasons), a cable was laid from the city of Baltimore to the Supreme Court Chamber in the Capitol Building in New York. Everyone in the Chamber held their breath, wondering if the whole thing was a waste of time. Morse tapped out a series of dots and dashes that transmitted all the way to Baltimore. There was silence in the great Chamber but not for long. An identical series of dots and dashes arrived back and was printed out on a paper ribbon in order that those gathered in the Supreme Court Chamber could see for themselves. And the message? It was from the Bible. 'What hath God wrought!' or, to put it in modern words, 'What a wonderful thing God has done!'

'It's God's work,' Samuel Morse said. 'He alone could have carried me through all my trials and enabled me to triumph over all the obstacles.'

And, in 1872, God carried him home to heaven.

Fact: Uses of Morse Code
Morse code can be used to help severely disabled people communicate. If they have a minimal control of movement they can use Morse code while blowing and sucking on a plastic tube. People with severe motion disabilities, who are also deaf and/or blind, can receive Morse code through a skin buzzer. Through the use of this code and modern technology, disabled people can obtain access to the Internet and electronic mail. Stroke sufferers have been known to communicate with Morse code by blinking their eyes. Prisoners of War have even used Morse code in this way to pass on secret messages while they were being shown on T.V. by their captors.

Keynote: Samuel first thought of using electricity to pass on information after having suffered a great tragedy in his life. He realised that, if he had been able to get in touch with his family, it may have been possible for him to be at home with his wife before she died. Sometimes good things do result from painful and tragic events.

Think: Some people might look on the death of Jesus Christ as just a tragic event. Jesus' suffering certainly was awful. But why do Christians celebrate the death of Jesus Christ and remember that day by calling it Good Friday? This is simply because Jesus' death freed his people from the power of sin and hell. It is through his death that sinners can be saved.

 Prayer: Thank you, Lord Jesus, for your death on the cross. Show me my sin so that I will realise I need to repent and turn to you for forgiveness.

George Washington Carver

'Goodness gracious me! What do we have here in the barn this early in the morning but a boy, and a hungry one at that.'

George looked set to run away.

'Don't go, boy,' the kindly woman said. 'At least wait and have your breakfast with us.'

The thought of food made up George's mind.

'Thanks, Ma'am,' he answered. 'I'm mighty grateful to you.'

Over breakfast the boy told his story.

'My dad and mum were slaves in a plantation near Diamond Grove. I never knew my dad. Some say he was killed in an accident hauling logs just after I was born.'

'Poor boy,' cooed the woman. 'You'll have another piece of warm bread.'

George took the bread and talked as he ate.

'When I was just a lil' tiny baby raiders carried off my mother and me as well as some others from the plantation. Mum held me fast and wouldn't let me go. But the Master came and traded me back, so I never saw my mother again.'

'If that's not the worst story I ever heard,' breathed the woman. 'To lose both your father and mother before you could remember them is a fearful bad start to a boy's life. What happened to you after that?'

George, who by now was warm and comfortably full, relaxed.

'The Master's name is Carver, and they call me Carver's George, for I ain't got no other name that I know of. He was good to me and treated me kind. I called them Uncle Moses and Aunt Sue.'

'Did you work for them?'

'No,' the boy admitted, 'not exactly work. Because I had neither father nor mother to keep me at it I spent most of my time exploring the world around me. The Master didn't seem to mind. He called me the Plant Doctor because I knew so much about the plants that grow around Diamond Grove.'

'You mean you heal the sick with your plant concoctions?' asked the woman, fascinated by what she was hearing.

'No,' he laughed, and his white teeth showed bright against his dark brown skin. 'I mean if there's anything wrong with growing things, I usually know how to help them grow better.'

'But if your master treated you kind, why've you run away?'

'I ain't run away,' George explained. 'Years past someone gave me a spelling book and I taught myself to read. Now I want to go to school. Master said I could leave and that the nearest school was at Neosho, eight miles away. So I packed my things in this bandana and I'm on my way to school.' There was a pause and then his voice grew quieter. 'But when I came last night it was too dark to find the school, so I found your barn instead. Thank you kindly, Ma'am, for the use of it.'

'I think you can call me Aunt Mariah, everyone does. And you don't have far to look for the school for there's one especially for black children on the other side of the fence.'

George's eyes opened wide in surprise.

'And,' said Aunt Mariah, who could sum up a situation in less time than most, 'you could do worse than be my house boy when you're not at school.'

On his first day at school, when asked his name, the boy did a quick turnaround. Instead of saying he was Carver's George, he gave the name George Carver.

'And what age are you?' he was asked.

'I don't rightly know,' the boy replied. 'But I'm told I might be ten. I think I was born in 1864.'

'I don't know what you did at the Carvers' place,' said Aunt Mariah, after George went to live in her home. 'But while you're here you'll join us in reading the Bible, in praying and in singing to the Lord. There's no real joy to be found in anyone else but Jesus. Seeing as you can read, I've a gift for you. Here, boy.'

George took the Bible from her hand and held it as the treasure it was.

'Why, thank you, Aunt Mariah,' he said, not knowing whether to laugh or cry. 'Sorry,' he spluttered, wiping tears from his eyes, 'I just ain't that used to getting presents.'

George served the good woman as a house boy while studying at Neosho school. Then he moved away to further his education. He was about twelve or thirteen years old, though George never did know his birthday.

Not long after leaving Aunt Mariah, the teenager saw something he was never to forget. He saw a black prisoner being beaten to death and his body burned in a fire. George, who was as dark-skinned as that poor prisoner, ran away from the terrible scene until he could run no longer. But he knew, even then, that he would never be able to run away from the memory of it.

The next time he saw Aunt Mariah he was a successful businessman who had sold his laundry business to pay to go to university.

'Goodness, gracious me!' the good woman said, when she heard his story. 'And you've come all the way back here to tell me. God bless you. Now, let's get to what's even more important. Are you following Jesus?'

Smiling widely, the young man assured Aunt Mariah that he certainly was. 'And I've you to thank for that,' he concluded.

'Don't thank me for anything, George Carver. Everything good comes from God.'

From Aunt Mariah's home, George went to Diamond Grove to tell Master Carver that he had gone to school and that he was now on his way to university. But when he arrived at the university a terrible disappointment was in store. At the sight of his black face, he was told, 'We take only Indians here, no blacks.'

It was not until he was thirty years old that George became a university student, and it was at Simpson College, a Christian university in Indiana, Iowa. That was in 1894. A minister who befriended the young man persuaded him to put that nasty experience behind him and to become a student after all. Unlike the previous university, he was welcomed by the white students and made to feel at home among them.

'What a beautiful painting!' a teacher said, when he looked at George's work. 'That flower is exquisite.'

'Thank you, Sir, but it's just a poor copy of a lovely thing the Lord has made.'

'A poor copy it is not. In fact, I've never seen finer botanical painting. I can almost smell the scent from the bloom.'

'Thank you kindly, Sir. And I thank the Lord for all the good things that grow.'

'Would you let us exhibit your paintings?' George was asked, some time later.

He took a little persuading but eventually four were sent to an exhibition in Cedar Rapids. All four were selected for the World's Columbian Exposition in Chicago.

'George,' said the College Principal, 'you could become a world-class botanical artist. You have a great gift.'

'Sir, I thank you for that, I really do, but I don't believe that's what the Lord wants me to do with the rest of my life.'

'What do you think you should be doing?' he was asked.

'I believe the good Lord wants me to become an agricultural scientist. That's not so far distant from being an artist. You know, it takes the same eye for detail.'

'Whatever you do, you'll do it well,' the Principal said, shaking George's hand.

After further training, George was appointed as Director and Consulting Chemist on the Agricultural Experiment Station of Tuskegee Institute in 1897.

'My job title is three times longer than my name,' said George, who by then called himself George Washington Carver.

The Tuskegee Institute was founded in 1881, by a black man for his own people. The founder, Booker Washington, 'wanted his fellow blacks to be of such practical and social value that even white people would come to feel that blacks were necessary for the happiness and well-being of the community.'

If that was the aim of Tuskegee Institute, Professor George Washington Carver was just the right person to employ. After all, even as a child he was known as the Plant Doctor. Everyone, no matter what their colour, needs to know how to grow their crops.

'Can you give me advice?' he was asked over and over again. And the problem was often the same. Poor farmers worked poor soil and both the farmers and the soil just grew poorer.

'Your soil is like a workman,' George told them. 'You need to feed it and rest it to get it to work for you. The problem is that because you're growing the same crop on the same land every year it has used up all the nutrients in the soil and there's nothing left to help the next crop grow.'

'That makes sense,' a farmer agreed. 'But it's always been cotton that's grown in these parts in the past.'

111

'It is,' George agreed, 'but it needn't always be in the future.'

Weekly lectures were arranged at which Professor Carver spoke about rotating crops instead of growing the same ones on the same fields, and about the composition of the soil, and how to decide what would grow best on the kind of soil each farmer had.

'For example,' he said, 'if you have three fields, try growing three crops, say sweet potatoes, peanuts and cotton one year. The following year grow the same crops but put the sweet potatoes in the peanut field, and so on, and the next year use that field for cotton.'

'Bring in a soil sample,' he told them, 'and I'll analyse it for you. If you know the kind of soil you have, you can work out the best crops to grow. Not every crop likes every kind of soil.'

At first only black farmers brought samples of their soil. As time passed, however, their crops were so much improved that white farmers started to brings theirs too. Then a strange thing happened. George's scientific farming methods were so successful that one year the farmers had such heavy crops of sweet potatoes and peanuts that they couldn't find buyers for them.

'What will we do?' the farmers asked. 'Everyone has enough of their own, and the shops just don't want any more.'

'Give me time, please,' George said. 'Let me talk it over with the Lord.'

Going into his laboratory at the Tuskegee Institute, George told his Heavenly Father all about the problem. Then he sat down and thought very, very hard. As he scribbled idea after idea, the pages of his notebook began to fill up. He was able to give the farmers ideas about other ways to use sweet potatoes and peanuts. By the end of his life he had found 300 different uses for peanuts and 150 new uses for sweet potatoes!

'If you can grow the crops,' he told the farmers, 'there will always be a use for them.'

'One day I went into my laboratory and asked God to tell me what the universe was made for,' he told an audience, who thought that was a strange thing to pray. 'And God said in my heart that I was asking for knowledge that my little mind could not possess. So I asked God what man was made for, and he still told me that the answer was too big for me.'

Some of his audience smiled, thinking this was a joke.

'Then I asked the Lord what the peanut was made for, and God told me how to turn it into shampoo, vinegar, coffee, printer's ink, milk, butter, salads, face powder, a cure for dandruff, soap and many other things besides. You see,' he concluded, 'until now we have always thought that the great Creator gave us three kingdoms: the animal, the vegetable and the mineral. Now he has added a fourth – the synthetic. That shows us how one thing can be made into something quite different. Think of it. From peanuts we get butter – peanut butter.'

'Did I hear that your fame has travelled all the way across the Atlantic?' a farmer asked him one day in 1916. 'I read in the paper that you'd been elected a Fellow of the Royal Society of Arts of Great Britain. Congratulations!'

'Thank you, Sir,' said Professor Carver, in his usual kind and humble way. 'But I only discover what the good Lord has made.'

Seven years later, in 1923, George was recognised in his homeland, when he was awarded the Springarn Medal by the Attorney-General of Kansas.

'The wonder of the medal is that it marks the contribution that the black population has made to national prosperity,' George was told by one of his fellow professors. 'And that's just what Tuskegee is all about. Would you ever work anywhere else?' he asked his friend.

George Washington Carver smiled. 'I've been offered other positions but I've never taken them. This is where I believe God wants me to be.'

Sadly, towards the end of George's life, race relations were the cause of much sorrow in the United States of America. When he wanted to see the flowers in a park in Montgomery, George had first to check if there was a sign forbidding black people from entering. There didn't seem to be one. So that humble gentleman went in to look at the flowers God had made. Seeing him, the park keeper rushed up to where he was and shouted, 'What are you doing here? Don't you know blacks ain't allowed? Get out!'

But, in 1943, when George Washington Carver died and went to heaven, he heard the gentle voice of Jesus welcoming him home.

Fact: $1,000,000
George Washington Carver declined an invitation to work for a salary of more than $100,000 a year (almost a million today) to continue his research on behalf of his countrymen. Carver did not patent or profit from most of his products. He freely gave his discoveries to mankind. Most important was the fact that he changed the American South from being a one-crop land of cotton to being multi-crop farmlands, with farmers having hundreds of profitable uses for their new crops.

Keynote: Carver did not profit from his products. 'God gave them to me,' he would say about his ideas, 'How can I sell them to someone else?' In 1940, Carver donated his life savings to the establishment of the Carver Research Foundation at Tuskegee, for continuing research in agriculture. This should remind us in a very small way of Jesus Christ who gave up the glories of heaven to come to earth to suffer and die to save sinners.

Think: What do you think makes a job or career worthwhile? Is it the salary? Is it the prestige or importance? Is it that you have to be clever before you can do that career or that you have to be physically strong? It is wrong to think of someone as more important because of their job or how much they earn. Remember that whatever you have you have because God gave it to you. We have no right to be proud in our own abilities when they have been given to us as a gift. But we must work hard to make the most of these abilities and to use them for God's glory.

Prayer: Dear Lord, help me to appreciate others for the variety of jobs they do. Help me not to be proud in myself but to be thankful for your gifts. Thank you, Lord, for all your people who work to bring glory to you and help to others.

C.T. Studd

'Keep your back straight, and push your feet forward in the stirrups,' said the groom, on C.T. Studd's first hunt.

C.T. did exactly as he was told.

'Now, let's see the three of you,' said Mr Studd, striding up to where his young sons were waiting to go on the hunt. This was C.T.'s first time, and he was just six years old. Two of his brothers, J.E.K. and G.B., were with him. They had names (Charles, Kynaston and George), but they were still quite young when they came to be known by their initials.

The boys looked very smart in their hunting gear, even though they had to be strapped on to their mounts because they were so small.

The Master raised the hunting horn to his lips, blew hard … and they were off, their hounds racing along beside them.

'I think the Studd boys were born in saddles,' the groom told his wife, as he described the chase to her that evening.

'They're game for anything,' she agreed.

'That's just as well,' laughed her husband, pulling off his riding boots, 'for the Leicestershire fences are reckoned to be the stiffest in England. It's a pity that Salamander's win was before the boys were old enough to enjoy it,' the groom thought aloud.

'Maybe 1866 won't be the only year that one of Mr Studd's horses wins the Grand National,' said his wife.

The groom shook his head. 'None of the horses he owns just now has what it takes.'

His wife laughed, 'Remember what you called Salamander when the horse first came here? An exhausted scarecrow!'

Hallaton Hall, in Leicestershire, was not to be home for much longer, as they moved shortly afterwards to Wiltshire.

'You bowl,' J.E.K. said, 'and I'll bat first.'

C.T. rubbed the ball in his hands and polished it on his trouser leg before running and taking the stump with a better overhand ball than most boys his age could manage.

'Getting some practice?' Mr Studd asked.

'Just trying out the new ground,' J.E.K. laughed. 'It's really good.'

On moving to Wiltshire Mr Studd had decided to have one of his paddocks made into a cricket ground, and a very good one too.

J.E.K. said, 'Thanks for doing this, Dad.'

Mr Studd smiled. He had made a large amount of money working in India, and now it gave him great pleasure to spend it – especially on horses and his new cricket ground.

'Will we take part in the country-house cricket this year?' C.T. asked his father.

'I think we should let the ground settle for a year then organise matches and cricket weeks as from the beginning of next season.'

When C.T. was thirteen years old his father became a Christian. As Mr Studd realised that horse racing and betting went hand in hand, he sold most of his racehorses. Three of the best ones were given to his oldest sons for hunting. Then he cleared one of the largest rooms in his very grand house and had it made into a room for Christian meetings. Life was changing for the Studd family.

One of Mr Studd's friends asked C.T. 'Are you a Christian?'

The boy tried to dodge the issue. He was home from boarding school to play cricket, not to discuss religion! But the man persisted and talked for a while about Jesus Christ. Later that day C.T. asked the Lord to be his Saviour. But he didn't tell his two brothers what had happened.

'Dear Father,' he wrote, when he was back in his room at Eton, one of the most famous schools in England. 'I am writing to tell you that I have become a Christian. I know that is what you've been praying for.'

A few days later, a letter arrived from Mr Studd to his three sons.

'My dear boys, I'm so delighted that you've all become Christians. Praise the Lord!'

As the boys passed the letter to each other their faces broke into smiles. Each had written to tell their father of their conversion, but they had been too embarrassed to tell each other. All three had become believers on the very same day. Just two years after his conversion Mr Studd died.

C.T., J.E.K. and G.B. all went on to play cricket for Cambridge.

'Did you hear the result of the Cambridge versus The Gentlemen of England match?' one don asked another.

'What was it? Did the Studds do us proud?'

'They did indeed. We won fair and square, with the three brothers making 249 out of a total of 504.'

'You don't get better than that,' laughed the don.

But things did get better than that.

'Congratulations on being picked for the English team,' said J.E.K. 'We'll be at the Oval* cheering you on.'

C.T. grinned. 'I'll be needing it.'

It was 1882, C.T. was 20 years old ... and

* The Oval: The U.K. national cricket ground.

England lost. A few days later the following mock obituary appeared in a newspaper.

In Affectionate Remembrance of English Cricket, which died at the Oval on 28th August, 1882. Deeply lamented by a large circle of sorrowing Friends and Acquaintances. R.I.P.

N.B. – The body will be cremated and the ashes taken to Australia.

The following year C.T. was in the Test Team that went to Australia to even the score. They won! A number of Melbourne ladies put some ashes into a small silver urn and gave it to Ivo Bligh, the English Captain. Some believe that they were the ashes of the ball used in one of the games, or of the bails*. While no one knows for sure, England and Australia still play for the 'Ashes' in the 21st Century.

'I'm ashamed of myself,' C.T. said. 'I've been a Christian for six years, and I've kept it to myself instead of sharing the good news of Jesus. As a result my faith has grown cold.'

But it was not to remain like that. Two old ladies were faithful in prayer for C.T. Studd and God answered their prayers. When G.B. was so ill that he was thought to be dying, God brought C.T. back to his senses.

'Will you come and hear Mr Moody?' he asked his friends a short while later.

*Bails: The small wooden bars placed on top of cricket stumps.

It was through the American preacher, D.L. Moody, that C.T.'s father had become a Christian. Several young men went with C.T., and a number were converted.

'When Mr Moody left for England,' he said later, 'I wanted to know what my life's work for the Lord Jesus Christ was to be. I wanted only to serve him, and I prayed for God to show me.'

God did show C.T. Studd what he wanted him to do. In fact, he showed seven young men at Cambridge that he wanted them to serve him in China with the China Inland Mission. They became known as the Cambridge Seven. In February 1885, the Cambridge Seven sailed for China.

'We have the length of our voyage to learn to be Chinese,' one of them said, as they sailed.

'Having our hair in a pigtail will seem strange at first, I'm sure. And so will wearing Chinese clothes.'

'I doubt that anyone will ever seriously think I'm Chinese,' laughed C.T. 'I'm far too tall.'

'Then you'll just have to shrink as we cross the China Sea. For China Inland Missionaries have to live as like the Chinese people as they possibly can.'

'Shanghai, April 1, 1885,' C.T. wrote at the top of his mother's first letter from China.

After telling her about a meeting the previous evening, he went on, 'I have been laughing all day at our grotesque appearance. Stanley, Monty and A.P.T. have been converted into Chinamen. We put on the clothes this morning, then were duly shaved and pigtailed. The other three had their moustaches off – they look so funny.'

The following three months were spent travelling 1,800 miles by the Yantse and Han Rivers to where they were to work. And they worked very hard indeed, serving the Chinese people and telling them about the Lord.'

'Now that I'm twenty-five,' said C.T. in December 1887, 'I'm due to inherit my share of my father's money. And what a wonderful time I'm going to have giving it away.'

C.T. believed that he should not keep his fortune for himself, and that the Lord would provide for his needs. His father had left him £29,000 – an absolutely huge sum of money at that time. 'I'll give £5,000 to Mr Moody, £5,000 to Mr Müller for his orphan and mission work, £5,000 to help the poor in London, and £5,000 for the work of the Salvation Army in India. I owe that money to India. That's where Father made his wealth.'

'What will we do with the money that's left?' he asked his wife-to-be.

Priscilla smiled. 'Charlie,' she said. 'What did the Lord tell the rich young man to do?'

'Sell all he had,' C.T. replied.

'Well then, we'll give it all away, then start clear with the Lord at our wedding.'

That's exactly what they did. God gave them what they needed every day for the rest of their lives. Once, when money was short, C.T. said, 'Funds are low again, hallelujah! That means God trusts us and is willing to leave his reputation in our hands.'

'Life is not easy,' Priscilla admitted in a letter home. 'For the past five years we've not gone out the door without being called foreign devils, and sometimes we are spat on by the people for whom we care so much.'

Nor was it easy for them as a family. They had five children when they were in China, four girls and a boy. Their little son died when he was just one day old. Not only that, but C.T., who suffered from asthma, seemed to be getting worse as time went on.

'We believe the Lord is calling us back to England,' C.T. and Priscilla told the China Inland Mission in 1894.

'Our work on the way out was to learn to be Chinese,' Priscilla said, when the matter had been decided. 'On the way home our work will be to try to teach the children some English. They don't know a word of the language.'

But that was just the beginning of the Studd girls learning a new language for, six years later, the Lord called their parents to be missionaries in India.

'My father wished that one of his children would take the good news about the Lord Jesus back to India, where he worked when he was young,' C.T. explained to his daughters. 'It was his way of thanking the Indian people.'

'Are we going to stay in this part of India for ever?' his youngest daughter asked. 'I like it here at Tricot.'

But six months later they were on the move. C.T.'s asthma was especially bad and it was thought the climate of Ootacamund in South India would suit him better. For the next five years he was minister of the Union Church in Ootacamund and the Studds saw many people become Christians.

'How happy father would have been,' C.T. thought, as he watched the church fill.

Just a short time later C.T. and his wife were the happiest parents of all. All four of their daughters became Christians and were baptised on the very same day.

'This is goodbye to India,' Priscilla thought, as the coast of the land she had grown to love faded into the far distance. 'I wonder if it's also goodbye to overseas missionary service.'

For a few years it seemed that was the case, though C.T. Studd travelled far and wide speaking at meetings. Many people went to hear him, who knew him as a famous cricketer rather than a Christian. And some who went to hear about the Ashes came away having put their faith in the Lord Jesus Christ. As they listened to C.T. speaking about Jesus, people realised that his enthusiastic spirit, which had made him throw everything into his cricket, now made him throw absolutely everything into serving the Lord.

'Cannibals want missionaries,' C.T. read in a Liverpool shop window in 1908.

Although he was severely asthmatic the Lord used that sign to call his servant to work in Africa. It took time, a great deal of planning, and hours and hours of prayer.

'It will mean you remaining in England while I'm there,' C.T. reminded Priscilla.

'I know,' she replied quietly. 'But if that's God's will he'll give us his strength.'

On 15th December 1910, C.T. sailed without Priscilla for Khartoum. After months of trekking through malaria and sleeping sickness country, C.T. knew where his heart lay.

'In the Congo, between the Nile and Lake Chad, there are so many people who have never heard of Christ. I believe that God wants me to spend the rest of my life here telling them about his Son Jesus.'

Although it was hard for Priscilla, she also wanted the Lord's will more than she wanted her own. And it was a comfort to her that when C.T. came home to England for a time, he took one of their daughters back with him to be a missionary and to marry a missionary.

'The work will go on after we've gone home to heaven,' she thought, as she prayed day after day for the land of Congo.

After twelve years of sacrificing time together, Priscilla spent two weeks with her husband at Ibambi, where he worked in the Congo.

'Look how they love one another,' people said, when they saw the couple together. 'They must love us very much indeed for Bwana Mukubwa* to stay here when his wife is thousands of miles away.'

That was the last time C.T. and Priscilla saw each other on earth. She died in 1929.

'Bwana Mukubwa has a busy day,' one of his Congolese friends said on Sunday 12th July 1931. 'Today's meeting will last many hours.'

The next day C.T. did not feel well, and the following Thursday he died and saw his wonderful Lord Jesus face to face.

* Big Boss

Fact: Cricket
Cricket's most likely birthplace is the Weald, an area of dense woodlands and clearings in South East England that lies across Kent and Sussex. The game was probably devised by children of the Weald's farming and metalworking communities. The game's origin seems to have been in Norman or Saxon times (i.e., before 1066). The original implements may have been a matted lump of sheep's wool as the ball; a crook or other farm tool as the bat; and a wicket gate or tree stump as the wicket.

Keynote: When C.T. Studd realised his funds were low one day he praised God because he realised that God trusted him. God knew that C.T. would trust him to provide. Perhaps you feel unsure about the future. Maybe you have worries and doubts. It is good to remember the lives of people like C.T. Studd. They are examples to us of how we should trust in God for all our needs – today and in the future.

Think: C.T. Studd wanted to know what his life's work for the Lord Jesus Christ was to be. He wanted to serve him. He prayed for God to show him what he should do. If you are wondering what the future holds for you, first make sure that your eternal future is secure. Trust in the Lord Jesus to save you from your sin. Then pray to God as C.T. did. Your life should be placed in his hand for today, tomorrow and eternity. He will show you what he wants you to do.

 Prayer: Lord Jesus, thank you that I can trust you always. Help me to trust in you for the future. I do not know what will happen but help me to follow you. Whatever I do – if I stay at home or travel to the other end of the world – may I do it for your glory. May I obey you in every area of my life.

John Bunyan

John watched his father at work and grinned. He liked to hear the clink, clink of his dad's metal tools against the pots and pans he was mending, for then he knew where his father was. When the clink, clink turned into a silence, John usually stopped whatever mischief he was up to and pretended to be the good son that John and Margaret Bunyan hoped he would be. But today his father, a tinker to trade, was busy and the noise of his mending went on for hours. Today John was free!

'Coo, coo' said John, from behind a bush.

His friends, who were passing by, recognised the signal and ducked behind the bush.

'You don't sound anything like a pigeon,' said one of the boys.

John didn't reply; he just aimed a kick in the right direction.

'Old Mother Taylor's apples are ready,' John told his friends. 'It's time for a feast.'

They knew that Mother Taylor was poor and hoped to sell apples to buy things she needed. That might have stopped some of the boys from stealing but it didn't stop ten-year-old John Bunyan. Because he was the ringleader the others did what he said. However, that year, 1638, the English summer had been so sunny that apples reddened on the outside before sweetening on the inside, and the boys suffered very sore stomachs.

'This place is a dump,' announced John, looking round the village of Elstow. 'As soon as I'm old enough I'm packing up my things and leaving here for good.'

'Going all the way to Bedford?' laughed an older boy. 'You'll make it there and back in time for your dinner.'

'Are you going away to London to make your fortune there?' teased another boy, who was much older and bigger than John. He wouldn't have teased him if they'd been the same size, for John could put up a good fight when he chose to.

'You could always be a lawyer,' laughed another. 'After all, you've been at school.'

A vision of his school days came into John's mind but he knew that he'd forgotten nearly everything he learned there. John Bunyan stuck out his tongue at his tormentors and ran off to find someone smaller than them to annoy.

'I'm going to tell Dad about you,' said John's younger sister Margaret. 'Everyone is talking about you. Old Mother Taylor told me you swore at her.'

'Don't you dare,' hissed the boy. 'Or I'll tell Dad things about you.'

'What things?' Margaret demanded.

'Things I'll make up,' laughed the boy. 'And they'll be worth a sore smacking!'

Margaret was right about John having a bad reputation. He was well known for his swearing and lying. In fact, mothers in Elstow told their young sons not to go near John Bunyan. He was a bad influence.

What people did not see was that deep inside himself John was a seriously disturbed boy. Dreams of hell upset him badly. He pictured demons and evil spirits bound up with chains for judgment, and he could just see himself among them. The sight of anyone reading the Bible or praying hit at John's heart so hard that he fought against it by doing something he knew to be wrong. Strangely, if he saw a person he knew to be a Christian doing something unkind, or saying something untrue, John was really upset. Poor boy, he really was in a mess.

'What's that moving in the grass?' one of his friends asked, as they walked near the village.

135

'It's an adder,' said John, picking up a stick to hit the snake.

His blow just stunned the creature. Seeing that, the young fool picked it up to do some showing-off.

'I'll teach this thing to be poisonous,' he said. And, holding the snake in one hand, he prized its mouth open and pulled out its fang with the other.

'You wouldn't catch me doing that,' said one of his friends.

'Too right,' added another.

In 1644, influenza swept through Bedfordshire. Hundreds of people were sick and death struck in many homes. John Bunyan's was one of them. First his mother died, then just a month later, his young sister died too. John was nearly sixteen years old but, when his mother and sister died in such quick succession, he must have felt for a while like a little lost boy.

'I told you I was going to leave Elstow,' John told his friends, 'and I'm going now.'

This was just weeks after the family's terrible sadness.

'I'm going to join Cromwell's Parliamentary Army.'

The English Civil War was raging at that time and John took sides with Cromwell against the King. Although Oliver Cromwell was a Christian, and each of his soldiers was given a Soldier's Catechism, young John Bunyan wasn't in the least interested.

'You're a very lucky young man,' his sergeant said one day.

'Don't I know it,' agreed John. 'That might have been me.'

'What happened?' asked a soldier, who was just passing by.

John told his story.

'I was meant to be going with some others to help in a siege. Just as we were preparing to leave, someone came and asked if he could change places with me. That was fine with me, so off he went. But–' he paused for effect – 'the poor man was shot in the head by a musket-ball and died. That was a lucky escape.'

'For you,' said the soldier, 'but not for him.'

For three years John fought with Cromwell's men and then he returned to Elstow, where he married. His first child, a daughter named Mary, was blind. John's wife had come from a Christian home and she had brought two Christian books with her when she was married. Although John's reading was poor, he ploughed his way through parts of them from time to time. His wife also sometimes persuaded him to attend church.

After the services, however, he forgot it was Sunday and went off to play sports with his friends. Once his minister preached on the commandment to keep Sunday special. John was very impressed ... right until after he'd had his lunch .... then he headed off to his sports again. During the game, it was as though God spoke directly to John. He dropped his bat and felt ashamed of himself. But, just as suddenly, he decided that he was so bad that God couldn't save him. Picking his bat up again, he played furiously till the end of the game.

From then on, John Bunyan's life was a total confusion. One day he wanted to learn about the Lord, the next he decided God couldn't possibly be interested in him. He tried for a time to live a good life; he even studied the Bible and his wife's Christian books. But he knew he wasn't a believer, and he was still scared of judgement.

'You coming to bell-ringing tonight?' John was asked, as he walked home from work one day.

Bell-ringing was one of his hobbies.

'I'll be there,' he said. 'Try and stop me.'

But that night he felt uncomfortable. What if one of the bells fell down on him? He knew he wouldn't go to heaven if he died.

'I'll stand here and ring the bell,' he said, pulling himself back against the wall.

The other bell-ringers looked at him with amused expressions.

As he walked home, it occurred to him that next time he went bell-ringing the steeple might fall down on top of him.

'That's it,' he decided. 'No more bell-ringing for me.'

Not long afterwards John, who was by now a tinker like his father, went off to Bedford to work one day.

'Look at them,' he thought, 'they've nothing better to do than gossip.'

As he drew nearer the little group of women, he realised they were talking about their faith. And they seemed to be saying that the Lord Jesus was their Saviour and Friend. John, who never hesitated to burst into other people's conversations, listened to the poor ragged women and wondered about their joy and grace. From then on he looked for excuses to work in Bedford just in order to hear what these women were saying.

'I think that young man is seriously looking for God,' one of the women decided and the others agreed.

'You should meet our minister, John Gifford,' they told him, when he next came along their road. 'He'll help you find Jesus.'

What a surprise it was to John to discover that Mr Gifford had once been as wicked as himself, having gambled, drank and spoken against the Lord for years before becoming a Christian. The two men became firm friends and twenty-five-year-old John Bunyan, tinker and troublemaker, became a believer in the Lord Jesus Christ. He was the talk of Bedford and Elstow yet again, but this time for the very best of reasons.

In 1655, John Gifford died, having lived long enough to hear his friend preach the gospel. John Bunyan became well known for his preaching. Because he had been so well known in the area before – for bad reasons – people went to hear him and were amazed at the change in the man. And how different life was in his home than it used to be. His wife, who by then had three children, must have praised the Lord for the change in her husband. Three years later, however, Mrs Bunyan died, just after their fourth child was born. It was a really hard time for John as he struggled to work as well as look after his four children. Over a year later he married again, and his new wife – Elizabeth – was a fine Christian woman.

After Cromwell's death, Charles II reigned as King of England.

'I promise that people will have liberty of conscience to worship as they see fit,' he said, and some people believed him.

Before long those whose consciences made them worship differently from the King found soldiers at their doors, and discovered what it was like inside prison cells.

'Will you use the King's Book of Common Prayer?' Elizabeth asked her husband.

'No,' he replied. 'I'll only use God's book, the Bible.'

The couple knew what that meant and were not surprised when trouble brewed.

It was November 1660, and John Bunyan was preaching at Lower Samsell, about twelve miles from their home in Bedford. When John arrived he discovered that a warrant had been issued for his arrest.

'I think we should cancel the service,' someone said.

'No, no,' said the preacher. 'I won't have the service cancelled just because of that.'

The service went ahead but was interrupted by a constable striding into the church and thrusting the warrant into John's hand. The following morning John found himself a prisoner in Bedford Jail. It was two months before he was called to answer to his charge. John finished his reply by saying, 'If I am out of prison today, I will preach the gospel again tomorrow – by the help of God.' Not surprisingly, Preacher Bunyan spent a very long time in prison.

While he was a prisoner, John worked on two things. He made leather laces to support his wife and children, and he began writing books. Of course, he was very well known, especially because he was in prison so long.

'If only the King thought about it, he'd set me free,' John said to his wife when she visited him. 'The longer he keeps me in prison, the better my books sell.'

Elizabeth, who supported her husband in all he did, smiled at the joke of it.

'It's quite true,' she said. 'The King keeps you here to stop you preaching the gospel, and because you're here you have time to write about the gospel.'

'Things seem more relaxed in the country now,' John said to a fellow prisoner, after twelve years spent mostly in prison.

'Do you think they'll set us free then?'

And that's just what happened. John Bunyan was released in 1672, and was free to preach for four years before being imprisoned again. It was in 1678 that his most famous book was published. *The Pilgrim's Progress* sold over 100,000 copies in its first ten years. It has never been out of print in all the years since then. It's second only to the Bible in the number of copies that have been sold. *The Pilgrim's Progress* is the story of a man called Christian who sets out to find his way to heaven. In many respects it's the story of

142

John Bunyan's life, as it describes the people who helped him and those who tried to hold him back. The names John chose for the characters and places in the book describe them well. There is the Giant Despair and Doubting Castle, among many others. *The Pilgrim's Progress* has since been translated into many different languages, rewritten for children, illustrated, published in cartoon form and made into films. In fact, there is a version of *The Pilgrim's Progress* for nearly every age of reader. John Bunyan could never have imagined that when he wrote it over 400 years ago!

Fact File: *The Pilgrim's Progress*

This book is an allegorical novel and is regarded as a great classic of literature. An allegorical story is a fictional story with a deeper and hidden meaning. *The Pilgrim's Progress* is about a man on a journey – but the deeper meaning is about how someone can get to heaven by believing in Jesus Christ. Some famous people who have read and enjoyed *The Pilgrim's Progress* include: The artist Vincent van Gogh; The preacher Charles Spurgeon; The poet Samuel Taylor Coleridge and The novelist John Buchan.

Key note: John Bunyan is described as a tinker and a troublemaker... but he was brought from being a trouble maker to being a preacher of God's Word. Jesus tells us in his Word that he did not come to save the righteous but to bring sinners to repentance. Jesus also tells us that it is not the healthy who need a doctor but the sick. We just have to realise that all have sinned and have fallen short of God's perfect standard. There is no one who is good – no not one.

Think: John Bunyan said, 'If I am out of prison today, I will preach the gospel again tomorrow.' Bunyan spent a long time in prison. The apostle Peter was also imprisoned for preaching about Jesus Christ. Peter was also told not to preach but he refused. The Pharisees and religious authorities could not stop these disciples of Jesus preaching about the One they loved. Where do you find it hardest to stand up for Jesus? If you were in prison for your faith how would the Bible help you to cope? Think about Christians who suffer for their faith in countries such as Afghanistan, Iraq, Myanmar and China. Pray for them and ask God to give you the courage and faith to stand up for Jesus Christ and his word.

 Prayer: Dear Lord, thank you for the example you give us. You suffered for us. Your love was so great that you were willing to die for us. Give us a love for you and your Word so that we can stand strong too. Help us to follow your example and forgive those who persecute us.

Quiz

How much can you remember about the ten boys who used their talents? Try answering these questions to find out.

Wilfred Grenfell

1. What was the name of the American preacher that Wilfred went to listen to?

2. What was Wilfred once trapped on with his dogs?

3. What two areas did Wilfred work in - both of these are now part of the nation of Canada?

C.S. Lewis

4. Can you name the series of chronicles that C.S. Lewis wrote - and which became worldwide best sellers?

5. What was the name of the imaginery world that C.S. Lewis invented as a young boy?

6. What was C.S. Lewis travelling in when he believed in Jesus Christ for the first time?

James Clerk Maxwell

7.   What scientist did James Clerk Maxwell owe a lot to?

8.   Who should we look to through nature?

9.   What area of Scotland did James grow up in?

Ghillean Prance

10.   What castle could Ghillean and his mother see from the boat?

11.   What was Ghillean's favourite book when he was a boy?

12.   Where did Ghillean go on plant hunting expeditions?

Paul Brand

13.   What disease infected 500,000 people in 2005?

14.   What disease killed Paul's father?

15.   What country did Paul go to in 1943?

Johann Sebastian Bach

16.   What two instruments was Johann playing when he was seven years old?

17.   Who used to be a pupil at Johann's Latin Grammer school?

18.   What words did Johann use to sign all his work?

Samuel Morse

19.   Why did Samuel's father choose Yale College for his son?

20.   What did Samuel want to be before he became a scientist?

21.   What was the first coded message that Samuel Morse sent from the Capitol building in Washington to Baltimore?

George Washington Carver

22.   George's parents were slaves on a plantation. What was the name of that plantation?

23.   What did Aunt Mariah give George as a present?

24.   How many different uses did George discover for peanuts?

C.T. Studd

25. What sport did C.T. play for England?

26. Which other members of C.T.'s family became Christians on the same day as he did?

27. Why did C.T. believe that he should give away his fortune?

John Bunyan

28. What is the name of the jail where John Bunyan was kept in prison?

29. What two things did John Bunyan work at during his stay in prison?

30. Who was John Bunyan's military commander during the civil war?

How well did you do?

Turn over to find out...

Quiz Answers

1. D. L. Moody.
2. A sheet of ice.
3. Newfoundland and Labrador.
4. *The Chronicles of Narnia.*
5. Boxen.
6. The sidecar of a motorcycle.
7. Michael Farraday.
8. God.
9. Kirkcudbrightshire.
10. Dunvegan Castle.
11. Gilbert White's *Natural History of Selborne.*
12. The Amazon Rainforest in Brazil.
13. Leprosy.
14. Black water fever.
15. India.
16. Violin and Harpsichord.
17. Martin Luther.
18. 'To the glory of God.'
19. They based their education on the Bible.
20. An artist.
21. 'What hath God wrought,' or 'What a wonderful thing God has done.'
22. Diamond Grove.
23. A Bible.
24. 300.
25. Cricket.
26. His two brothers.
27. He believed that God would provide for his needs.
28. Bedford Jail.
29. Making leather laces and writing books.
30. Oliver Cromwell.

Author Information:
Irene Howat

Irene Howat is an award-winning author who lives in Scotland. She has published many biographical books for all ages and is particularly well-known for her biographical material. She has written many books about the lives of different Christians from around the world. She has also written a biographical work about her own life entitled: *Pain My Companion*. Irene has many other interests including painting, dog walking and editing her Church's young people's magazine called *The Instructor*.

Start collecting this series now!

Ten Boys who Didn't Give In
Polycarp, Alban, Sir John Oldcastle,
Thomas Cranmer, George Wishart
James Chalmers, Dietrich Bonhoeffer
Nate Saint, Ivan Moiseyev, Graham Staines
ISBN 1 84550 0369

Ten Girls who Didn't Give In
Blandina, Perpetua, Lady Jane Grey, Anne
Askew, Lysken Dirks, Marion Harvey,
Margaret Wilson, Judith Weinberg, Betty
Stam, Esther John
ISBN 1 84550 0369

Ten Girls who Used Their Talents
Anne Lawson, Selina, Countess of
Huntingdon, Mildred Cable, Katie Ann
Mackinnon, Sarah Edwards, Patricia St
John, Helen Roseveare, Harriet Beecher
Stowe, Mary Verghese, Maureen McKenna
ISBN: 1-84550-147-0

JIM ELLIOT: HE IS NO FOOL
Irene Howat

ISBN: 184550 0644

Jim Elliot and four other young men were in the middle of doing God's work when they were brutally killed, by the very people they had come to rescue. However, Jim had realised that there was nothing more important than Jesus and that was why he was there. These young men knew the dangers but still went ahead with their plans to reach out to the Auca Indians.

After their deaths the work carried on thanks to Jim's wife, Elizabeth Elliot and Nate Saint's sister, Ruth Saint. Many Auca Indians came to know Jesus Christ for themselves and the church is still growing in that area of Ecuador today.

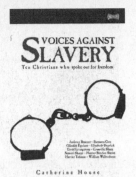

Voices Against Slavery
Catherine House

ISBN 1 84550 145 4

Over two hundred years ago human beings were bought and sold in the same way that animals were or sacks of flour. Although slavery is now banished in America, the U.K. and other western countries people are still bought and sold around the world. Today's slave markets are still the means used to destroy countless young lives.

In the 21st century as in centuries past Christians need to speak out against slavery. Catherine House introduces us to ten voices that spoke out for freedom. These men and women come from different times and different backgrounds but they have one voice – a Christian voice – a voice against slavery.

Anthony Benezet; Elizabeth Heyrick; Baroness Cox; David Livingstone; Granville Sharp; Harriet Beecher Stowe; Harriet Tubman; Olaudah Equiano; Samuel Sharpe; William Wilberforce.